CIVILIZATIONS OF BLACK AFRICA

CIVILIZATIONS
OF BLACK AFRICA

JACQUES MAQUET
University of California
Los Angeles

Revised and Translated by
JOAN RAYFIELD
York University
Toronto

New York
OXFORD UNIVERSITY PRESS
London   Toronto   1972

OXFORD UNIVERSITY PRESS

Oxford   London   Glasgow
New York   Toronto   Melbourne   Wellington
Nairobi   Dar es Salaam   Cape Town
Kuala Lumpur   Singapore   Jakarta   Hong Kong   Tokyo
Delhi   Bombay   Calcutta   Madras   Karachi

PREFACE

This book is not a survey. Though I have tried to omit nothing essential about African cultures, the relative importance placed on their various elements reflects a certain interpretation which will be explained later. The treatment does not follow a didactic method which sets out the same categories in the same order for each civilization (techniques, economy, kinship system, political organization, arts, etc.) but each of these categories will be illustrated as appropriate in the description of one or another of the civilizations.

Though I do not accept the evolutionary viewpoint according to which societies go chronologically through various cultural stages (such as: hunting, herding, agriculture; animism, polytheism, monotheism; polyandry, polygyny, monogamy), the first civilization treated, that of the bow, is the oldest one, and technically the simplest, while the last, the civilization of industry, is the most recent and enjoys the most advanced technology. This treatment enables me to set out each complex of institutions in the civilization of which it seems most characteristic, but does not mean that it is not present in the other civilizations which will be described later. Thus groups based on kinship are especially important in the civilization of the clearings in connection with which they are described, but they play a considerable part in the others; in the same way, hunting, which is the major means of subsistence in the civilization of the bow, persists as a secondary activity in the others.

Neither is this book a scientific treatise in which each statement of fact is footnoted with a citation of the source. The reader can, however, easily find the source: the names of the authors whose work I have used are mentioned in the text—their writings, in the bibliography. It is from these writings that the extracts in quotation marks are taken.

A work of synthesis is made possible only by all the research which has gone before it; I acknowledge my debt to the authors whose names appear, some of them several times, in this book.

To make things easier for the reader who is not familiar with the conventions of transcribing African words commonly used in writings in the social sciences, I have used English spellings for geographical or ethnic terms which have become part of the English language (thus, a Bantu, a Bantu language, Bantu dialects; a Zulu, a Zulu custom). In other cases I have kept official spellings, that is, those which have been authorized by national administrations (Bujumbura, Douala, Luanda); for names of languages, tribes and other social groups, I have used a simplified orthographic spelling (only characters used in English, without diacritical marks), words being reduced to their radical and without grammatical variations of form (a Kuba, not a Mukuba; Kuba women, not Bakuba women; the King of the Ganda; Ganda society); for common nouns denoting things or institutions, the same rule has been followed, but these words are printed in italics, (the *molimo*, a *garagu*). In phonetic orthography, *u* is pronounced as in *blue*, *e* as in *bed*, *s* always as in *sun*, *g* always hard as in *good*.

Jean-Claude Schalchli has collaborated with patience, skill, intelligence and friendship in this work, helping me to collect and make use of a vast mass of documents and assisting in all stages of the preparation of this book.

I am very grateful to Joan Rayfield for her competent revision and expert translation of the text.

The illustrations have been collected thanks to the kindness of many colleagues, both Africanists and photographers.

Los Angeles   J.M.
November 1971

CONTENTS

THE CIVILIZATION OF THE CLEARINGS

THE CIVILIZATION OF THE GRANARIES

THE CIVILIZATION OF THE SPEAR

THE CIVILIZATION OF CITIES

THE CIVILIZATION OF INDUSTRY

PHOTOGRAPHS

PHOTOS BY JACQUES MAQUET

MAPS

MAP DESIGN BY DAVID LINDROTH

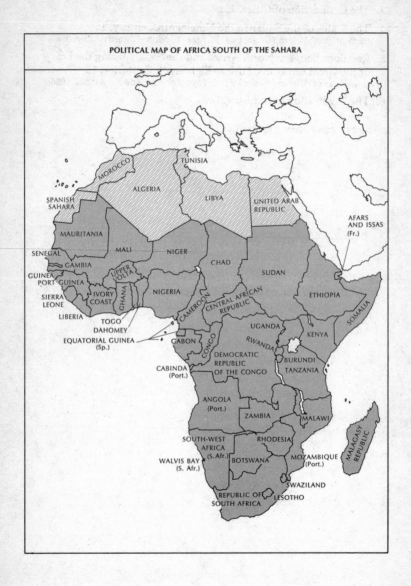

POLITICAL MAP OF AFRICA SOUTH OF THE SAHARA

INTRODUCTION

Art is not a universal language that all may clearly read. Works of art produced in our own society are often obscure to us, even those which move us, which we love passionately or violently hate. For communication is established at a level of personality deeper than the intellect, in an inner center where understanding is more global. What is lost in precision, in conceptual and verbal expression, is gained in immediacy and intensity. The men and women of Africa have ways of feeling, thinking and behaving that seem strange to us, sometimes very strange. By living in the intimacy of an African community, a Westerner can enter into its world. But this precious experience can hardly be obtained more than two or three times in the lifetime of one individual, even if he is an anthropologist.

Of course a culture may be approached in other ways than by intuitive participation. It can be unraveled and its various aspects may be described and analyzed by conceptual and discursive means. These, in fact, are the means that have been used throughout this book. But in order to appreciate to the fullest the inner experience of a culture, to understand the inside of African ways of life, we must take a long look at the works produced by Black artists. But do we look at this art with the same eye as the African for whom it was made? No! replies Chris Marker, "we look at it as if its justification for its existence lay in the pleasure it gives us. And we find visual beauty where a member of the Black community sees the face of a culture." It is true that most African works of art have a function in the society from which they arose that is different from the one they have in the West. In Africa, they are the king's sceptre, the chief's stool, the initiator's mask, the warrior's spear; here they are museum objects, pieces in a collection, pictures in expensive books. It is also true that the knowledge of an object's meaning in its own culture is not without effect on one's aesthetic appreciation of it. But the language of forms, when it is perfect, can make itself understood across cultural barriers. Through the balance and rhythm of masses and surfaces, basic universal emotions are expressed and understood and thus shared by the foreign viewer. Such are the feelings aroused by the human condition, such as man's weakness and his subjection to nature, the joy of fertility and the sadness of growing old, the strength of authority and the humility of subjects, the glory of wealth and the dependence of ordinary people, calm wisdom and resigned solitude, the survival of the group and the death of the individual. Through the rhythm of the masses of a Baule statuette, a non-African sees feminity as much as Léopold Sédar Senghor, who writes of it: "Two themes of sweetness sing in counterpoint. Ripe fruits of the breasts. The chin and the knees, the haunches and the calves are also fruits or breasts. The neck, the arms and the thighs, columns of black honey." Faced with a work produced in a certain society to serve a given function, a man from a different civilization, not knowing the exact use of the object, may still feel an emotion very similar to that which the artist expressed in his forms. This shared experience is probably the only possible communication between men separated by time, space, language, habits of life and thought. And this communion may produce an immediate understanding of the special feeling of a culture.

On the threshold of examining each civilization, we shall contemplate some of the works of art it has produced.

CIVILIZATIONS OF BLACK AFRICA

Settlement of railway workers, Rhodesia

Colonial African district near a European town, Butare, Rwanda

Street in Zaria, northern Nigeria

Contemporary monument in public square Mbarara, Uganda

Traditional suspension bridge, Congo-Brazzaville

CIVILIZATIONS

Societies and Cultures

With its solid land mass, almost unindented coastline, sharp separation from other lands by seas and oceans, Africa exactly fits the idea of a continent: a large section of the world the whole of which may be traversed without crossing the sea. Can the unity of Africa, so conveniently expressed by this geographical category, be translated into an equally simple and satisfying concept in the language of anthropology? When we are dealing with the groups of men who inhabit this continent and with their traditions, what conceptual tools will enable us to grasp their unity or unities? What are "continents" and "natural regions" for the anthropologist?

Society and culture, the two basic concepts of anthropology, define concrete units which must be our starting point. These terms are used here in their customary sense. A society is a group of persons whose activities as an organized whole suffice to ensure that the material and psychological needs of each of its members will be satisfied; its members regard themselves as forming a unit with well-defined boundaries. A culture is a complex totality of material objects, items of behavior and ideas, acquired in varying degrees by each member of a given society.

These two entities are mutually related: a society could not exist without a culture, a collective heritage handed down from generation to generation, which saves its members from having to re-invent all adaptations; a culture presupposes the existence of a group which gradually creates it, lives it out and communicates it. These are the elementary units which constitute the social reality of Africa: societies, each of which has its own cultural individuality, expressed by its own name.

The approach adopted in this book is that of anthropology. This discipline, which was not fully established until the second half of the nineteenth century, has for a long time been defined by its subject matter—non-literate societies—and by the research techniques necessitated by this subject matter—observations of behavior, oral questioning, etc., since the use of archives and written questionnaires was impossible. The contribution of anthropology in what we might call its ethnological stage to the scientific knowledge of social phenomena is certainly very valuable. For the concept of culture arose out of the opportunity of studying societies which differ from those of the West in that they are smaller in size, and simpler in their techniques. Ethnology broadened anthropological perspectives by showing that social organizations (kinship systems, political institutions, associations, etc.), if they are to be fully understood, must be considered in relation to other sections of their own culture: techniques, economy, ritual and philosophical ideas, arts and beliefs. The study of non-literate societies has greatly enriched our knowledge of man, but in the Africa of the second half of the twentieth century non-literate societies have become rare exceptions. Anthropology has gone beyond its ethnological stage and no longer confines itself to non-literate societies. This puts an end to the anomaly of defining a discipline by its subject matter rather than by its approach. The study of the social phenomena of non-literate groups is a special field (ethnology) rather than a discipline (anthropology). The fact that it was a separate discipline at a certain time reveals a probably unwitting racism.

There are many African societies. George P. Murdock lists almost 850. Obviously these socio-cultural unities must be grouped into a few broad categories so that they may be discussed within the limits of a book. But such groups must not be arbitrary; they must correspond to certain boundaries existing in social reality.

How should cultures be grouped? The broadest category is that which comprises all African cultures. Such a category was called "African civilization" by Leo Frobenius, and *négritude* by Léopold Sédar Senghor and the writers associated with the periodical *Présence Africaine*. Cultural features are sought which might be called characteristic of Africa and which distinguish it from the other cultural "continents" such as the Western world, the Indian tradition, Chinese civilization, Islam, etc. To the degree to which more similarities are found between the various cultures of Africa than between African and non-African cultures, it is justifiable to place the African cultures in a separate category. These attempts emphasize the most intellectual aspects of a culture: philosophy, myths and art forms, important symbols indeed, but they are not the only ones. Though it is interesting, in order to discover "the special quality of Africa," to contrast Africa with what is outside it, it is just as valid to consider Africa in itself and to try to discern the major cultural categories within it. It is this latter point of view which I adopt here.

Societies, which underlie cultures, are situated in space and time. In classifying them we must take account of these two dimensions. Darryl Forde's *Ethnographic Survey* of Africa classifies "peoples or groups of related peoples" on a purely geographic basis. One society (or, more often, a group of neighboring societies) is treated separately, and the resulting units are grouped into broad geographic regions—West Africa, East Central Africa, West Central Africa, etc., which in no way claim to represent cultural uniformities.

H. Baumann and D. Westermann emphasize the historical dimension. But this is historical reconstruction rather than history. They posit, as a starting point, nine basic African cultures, mother cultures, so to speak, purer and more coherent than those which could be observed in the nineteenth and early twentieth centuries. These cultures are actually "still present in superimposed layers, which may be separate or intermingled." The resulting composite cultures are called circles of civilization. Baumann and Westermann distinguish twenty-six of these. Their impressive work seems to be as good as their hypotheses concerning the cultural past of Africa.

The same may be said about the work of George Peter Murdock, which is equally impressive in its scope. Murdock attempts to describe the principal cultural developments and population movements which have occurred in Africa in the course of the last seven millennia, and to sum up what we know about the cultures of each of the regions based on this historical reconstruction.

The chief fault of classifications based principally on geographical or historical criteria is that they do not bring out sufficiently the specificity of the socio-cultural phenomenon. After all, since one's aim is to group together cultures which resemble one another, the basic criteria should be cultural, not spatial or temporal.

This problem gave rise to the culture area concept developed by Melville J. Herskovits. By "culture area" he means a region in which similar cultures may be found. The geographical framework is still very important in this concept, but it is subordinated to that of cultural resemblances. Applying this concept to Africa, Herskovits in 1924 suggested division of Africa into nine culture areas. He revised these several times; the last published version appeared in 1945. The cultures of each area have an all-over resemblance to one another. Thus the cultures of the East African Pastoral Area are all based on the high prestige value accorded to cattle, and this focus of interest characterizes the whole culture.

Herskovits's culture areas enable us to grasp the main cultural variations of Africa. I make use of them in this book, but place less stress on their spatial basis. I do not share his aim of setting out large areas each representing a single kind of culture. I give more importance to the time dimension and adopt a more precise hypothesis about socio-cultural structure.

In her study on African civilizations, Denise Paulme also takes an anthropological point of view but, unlike Herskovits, she gives considerable importance to historical depth. She chose to deal with historical and anthropological data separately; this gives her work great clarity. I attempt here to include this historical point of view in the cultural framework.

The Concept of Civilization

The actual cultures of Africa may be grouped into several *civilizations*. While each culture is bound up with a certain society which can be identified by its members—they know that they are Bambara and that the Bambara behave in a certain way and have certain customs—a civilization is not the tradition of a certain group, and those who participate in a civilization are not usually conscious of doing so. The task of marking the boundaries of civilizations falls on the anthropologist.

Each of these civilizations comprises what we believe to be common and essential to the various actual cultures which can be regarded as a broad group. The term "essential" refers to a certain hypothesis about the relative importance of the various aspects of a culture and the influence which these aspects exert on one another. It is impossible to classify cultures on the basis of their similarities without a master hypothesis such as this, which will indicate which similarities are significant and which are not.

Culture has been defined as being a social heritage. Looked at from another viewpoint, it is a system of adaptation of a group to its environment. Suppose that, by some accident, a generation did not hand down to the next one its collection of adjustments to an environment: the society would perish. The most urgent aspect of adaptation consists in extracting from the natural habitat that which is necessary to maintain the lives of individuals. This is why the production of material goods is the basis of any culture. This production depends on the natural resources offered by the habitat of a society, and the utilization techniques at the society's disposal. The other aspects of a culture—economic organization, political institutions, world view, art, etc.—can develop only within the limits set by production. This dependence of the totality of the culture on the relationship between its environment and its technology is especially noticeable in societies which live only just above the subsistence level. As this situation is common in Africa, African civilizations may be very adequately characterized by a certain type of material production. On the other hand, the more rudimentary the technology the greater the importance of the natural habitat. This explains why the spatial boundaries of certain civilizations coincide with those of natural regions having a certain type of vegetation or a certain climate.

This dependence of certain aspects of a culture on its means of production is not determinism. It is simply the case that a subsistence economy precludes certain political forms such as, for example, the state: how could a body of officials, devoting their full-time activities to administration, exist in a society in which each individual consumes as much as he produces? When the production of material goods provides a surplus, the possibilities of political forms increase.

Another factor works in the same way as this objective limitation of cultural possibilities by technology. This is the mechanism by which we construct our ideas and conceptions on the basis of our experience. After all, the Africans confront the world around them primarily in their work as producers. Starting from their experiences of effort, submission, anxiety and success in the work situation, they elaborate philosophical views about man and the world, religious and magical beliefs, rules of conduct. It is not surprising that the most intellectual levels of a culture reflect the material basis of that culture, mediated by everyday experiences.

When the material basis allows the establishment of a system of social stratification (we shall see how this happens when we study the civilization of granaries), the interests of a privileged group, that of the rulers, coincide with that culture's tendency to organize itself on the basis of its production techniques. This privileged group in effect has an interest in maintaining the economic and political systems which are to its advantage; it imposes, or at least favors, the ideology that corresponds to and justifies its situation.

If the three factors we have just mentioned—limitations set by productivity, projection of essential experience, maintenance of ideology by privileged groups—were operating in isolation, they would combine to form highly integrated civilizations, in which a technology closely bound up with a certain physical environment would be the foundation on which a lower level of economic and political institutions and then an upper level of intellectual and artistic creations would systematically develop. It would be simple if this were so, but unfortunately it is not.

First, the natural habitat or the technology may change. It has very often happened in Africa that a society migrates, and moves, for example, from the forest to the savanna, or that a new method of agriculture is borrowed from another group, or even that a new tool is invented or acquired. This change on the basic level will have repercussions on all levels of the culture, but sometimes the time lag may be quite long.

Civilizations of Black Africa

When all the processes have been taking place, perhaps over a period of centuries, in a society, its culture may present a very irregular, even chaotic appearance. However, by analyzing the culture we can attempt to discover the essential patterns. This is what I shall try to do in describing each of the great Black civilizations.

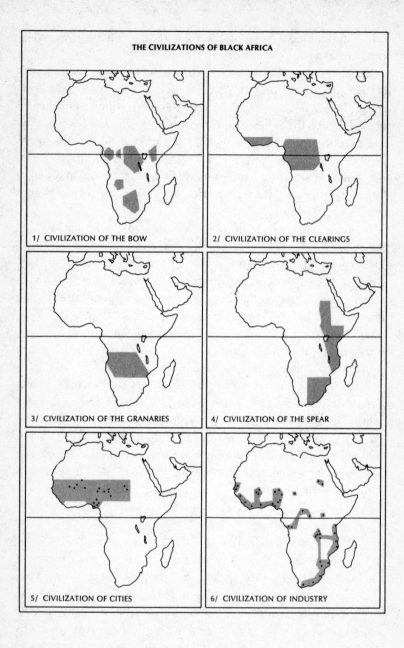

THE CIVILIZATIONS OF BLACK AFRICA

1/ CIVILIZATION OF THE BOW

2/ CIVILIZATION OF THE CLEARINGS

3/ CIVILIZATION OF THE GRANARIES

4/ CIVILIZATION OF THE SPEAR

5/ CIVILIZATION OF CITIES

6/ CIVILIZATION OF INDUSTRY

In this book I shall consider only those civilizations called Black African or sub-Saharan African; excluding on the one hand the societies and cultures to the north and the east of the Sahara, and on the other the European minorities established in various parts of Africa during the colonial period.

The division of Africa into two cultural areas, one north and one south of the Sahara, is arbitrary. The great desert, though in some respects a barrier, has also been a communication route, witness the map of caravan trails linking the Mediterranean coast to Niger and Chad. Islam, a religion with scriptures, is not confined to North Africa but extends widely south of the Sahara from coast to coast. The Nile valley was also a communication route between Black Africa and Egypt. The Cushite kingdoms of Axum and Meroe were a meeting point for a millennium, from about 700 B.C. to 400 A.D. At this time Meroe was conquered by the kingdom of Axum, thus extending communication as far as the Eastern Horn. If what is sometimes called White Africa is excluded from our study, it is not because it is a separate cultural world.

Neither are racial differences a reason for excluding it. Contrary to popular opinion, until quite recently no correlation, either positive or negative, could be discovered between a group's physical type and its cultural forms. Furthermore, race classifications at the present time are far from definitive. I include in this work the societies of the Pygmies and the Bushmen, who, from the biological point of view are not of negroid stock. However, I do conform to the convention of separating the two Africas (north and south of the Sahara). It is based on academic traditions which have split into separate fields the study of north and north-east Africa on the one hand and Black Africa on the other.

The European minorities of the colonial period were certainly of great importance as the agents of diffusion of the industrial techniques which form the base of the last of the Black African civilizations. In this way the European groups participated in the formation of one of the African civilizations, but we do not think that the cultures of these few, rare groups which have taken root in Africa should be considered separately from the industrial civilization. There is no colonial civilization. The consummation of the colonial period which occurred in our time leads us to exaggerate the importance of these few decades.

African Languages

Language is part of any culture. It is gradually transmitted to a child from his earliest infancy, it provides the categories through which the world is perceived, and it is the vehicle of teaching which enables people to learn other than by example.

African languages are bound up with African social reality. When a society lives in a rather isolated situation, its language too tends to become specialized. On the other hand contacts between groups spread their languages; and when several previously independent groups are subjected to a single political authority, the use of a single language tends to prevail. However, to a much higher degree than all other aspects of a culture, languages constitute systems which evolve according to their own laws of development. For this reason they are studied by a highly specialized discipline. This fact must explain why I am dealing with it very briefly at this point rather than in each of the chapters devoted to the great African civilizations.

First we must recall that there has existed for a long time a confusion between the race, language and culture as criteria for the classification of African phenomena. Thus the term "Bantu," which denotes a language family, has been used to designate a group of people with certain physical features in common, or a way of life based on agriculture, or even a philosophy. The same has happened to the term "Hamite" also a linguistic term, which has often been used as a synonym for pastoralist, or even for a tall, light-skinned individual. This might perhaps be justified if each of these groups constituted a racial unit, spoke a common language or related languages, and made its living from the environment in the same way. But such entities do not exist. The Fulani herdsmen do not speak a Hamitic language, the peoples of the Lake Chad region who speak Hamitic languages do not raise cattle, and the tall, light-skinned cattle herders of the Great Lakes region speak Bantu languages.

There are many African languages; estimates vary between 700 and 1500. Various classifications have been proposed by linguists. The most widely accepted is that of Joseph Greenberg, an American linguist.

Greenberg classifies African languages by a technique which he sets out in *The Languages of Africa* and *Essays in Linguistics*, chapter III. He takes a number of basic vocabulary items—words denoting concepts important in any culture, such as the names of parts of the body, numbers up to ten, words for the sun, water, etc.—of a group of languages which may possibly be genetically related. Comparisons of grammatical forms are also helpful, but vocabulary is most useful, because in the case of African languages word lists are sometimes all that the linguist has to work with; the technique is effective if only twenty or so items of basic vocabulary are available. He then compares the words for each concept in pairs or groups of languages which may be related. If he finds a number of cognates (words similar in form and meaning) in the languages he compares, and if the differences in form between the cognates show a regular pattern (e.g., Latin *pisces*, English "fish"; Latin *pater*, English "father", where a "p" sound in Latin regularly corresponds to an "f" sound in English) it may be assumed that the languages being compared have a common origin. (Some resemblances may be due to chance and some to borrowing—though such basic vocabulary items are seldom borrowed—but these would be insufficient to distort the general pattern.) In this way languages may be classified into groups according to the degree to which they resemble each other; and the groups may then be compared with each other to reveal that languages which appear to be unconnected may have a common origin in the more distant past. The

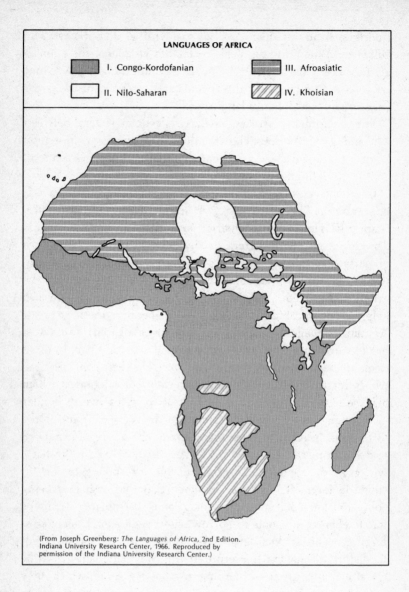

LANGUAGES OF AFRICA

I. Congo-Kordofanian
II. Nilo-Saharan
III. Afroasiatic
IV. Khoisian

(From Joseph Greenberg: *The Languages of Africa*, 2nd Edition. Indiana University Research Center, 1966. Reproduced by permission of the Indiana University Research Center.)

end result enables the linguist to discover the probable homeland of the mother language and the order in which speakers of that mother language left their homeland, taking with them the dialects which evolved into the daughter and granddaughter languages he is now studying.

Greenberg classifies the many hundreds of languages spoken in Africa into four large families; his classification corresponds in broad outline to those of earlier students of African languages, such as D. Westermann, and is generally accepted by modern linguists. These families are: *Khoisan*, the "click" languages, spoken by the Bushmen and Hottentots and some other peoples of south-western Africa and Tanzania. *Niger-Congo*, spoken over most of Africa south of a line drawn from Dakar to Mombasa. It comprises six main branches, one of the most important being the Benue-Congo branch, which includes the many and widely spoken Bantu languages. Another important branch is the West Atlantic, spoken in the south-western part of the "bulge" of Africa. Greenberg includes Fulani among the West Atlantic languages, though other specialists have had difficulty in establishing a relationship between Fulani and other African languages. Greenberg also groups Kordofanian with the Niger-Congo languages. *Nilo-Saharan*, spoken from the central Sudan to the Great Lakes region. It comprises six branches, including Songhai, and also Chari-Nile; the latter includes what some other linguists call the Nilotic languages. *Afroasiatic*, so called because it includes languages of north-west, north and north-east Africa as well as the Semitic languages of south-west Asia. This classification is based on four language groups, Semitic, Berber, ancient Egyptian and the Cushitic languages of East Africa. The Afroasiatic family has two main African branches, Chad (which includes Hausa, spoken in northern Nigeria) and the Cushitic languages now spoken in north-east Africa.

Until the beginning of this century African languages were unwritten. An exception is Swahili, the native language of certain peoples living in the coastal areas of Kenya. According to the

Russian linguist Olderogge, northern dialects of Swahili were written in Arabic script as early as the twelfth century. The oldest surviving manuscripts so far discovered are some letters and poems dating from the first half of the eighteenth century, when Swahili was already established as an important lingua franca, but the sophistication of these manuscripts suggests that Swahili had been written for a long time. Poetry is still written in Swahili in Arabic script, but for general purposes the Roman script has been used since the beginning of the twentieth century. This has enhanced the usefulness of Swahili as a lingua franca. It has been adopted as the official language of Tanzania. (All the other new African nations use the language of their former colonial occupants, usually French or English.)

During the latter part of the nineteenth century the Vai of Liberia devised an alphabetic script for their language, which is said to have developed from an earlier pictographic script. King Njoya of the Bamum in Cameroon, under the influence of Europeans or Hausa merchants, invented a script about 1895. It began with pictographs but soon became a syllabic script with a tendency towards alphabetization.

But these are rare exceptions. All other African languages were written only under the influence of colonial administrations and missionaries. News-sheets in African languages were important in some African countries in the early stages of nationalist movements. But nowadays literacy usually goes along with the use of one of the major languages of the world. It is still true that writing has played no part until the present century in the social or political history of Africa.

The Richness of African Languages

It is doubtful whether there are any characteristics which are common to all African languages and which distinguish them from non-African languages. (This is to be expected since we know that one of the super-families of African languages, the

Afroasiatic, is not confined to Africa.) However, many writers have commented on the richness of the resources of African languages, and this quality can be corroborated in many cases.

One manifestation of this richness is in vocabulary. Westermann mentions that the adjective "big" may be translated by 183 words in Nupe and 311 in Hausa. As Senghor points out, "there are ten, sometimes twenty words to designate an object according to changes in its form, weight, volume or color, and as many words to designate an action, according as it is single or multiple, weak or strong, beginning or ending."

This richness in vocabulary has been used to support the argument that it is impossible to express abstract ideas in African languages, and that this wealth of words conceals an intellectual poverty: the inability to generalize. It is enough for our purpose to point out here very briefly some elements which demonstrate the inaccuracy of this argument. Generalizing terms do exist in the vocabulary, but the aspect of perception selected as the basis for generalization is not always the same as that which has been chosen by European languages. Thus in Ewe the English words juice, milk, tears, wine, broth, pus, are translated by one word, *tsi*, which means "water" and has a determinant added; thus in Ewe the common characteristic of qualities designated by these six English words has been abstracted, and one speaks of fruit-water, breast-water, eye-water, palm-water, meat-water, wound-water. I do not know whether an Ewe would conclude from this that in English "the abundance of words is due to the fact that the speaker perceives in the world around him only independent items and rarely achieves the concepts of generalization and totality." This sentence is from Westermann, who, applying it to African languages, does not seem to have been aware of his ethnocentricity. In fact there exists in certain Bantu languages, in Rwanda for example, a prefix *bu-*, which indicates that the root must be understood in its abstract meaning: *mu-gabo*, man; *bu-gabo*, manliness.

On the grammatical level, this richness is displayed in a great complexity of forms. This exists not only in the Bantu and Sudanic languages, but also in the click languages. Thus Westermann reports that Nama, a Hottentot dialect, distinguishes the inclusive and exclusive in the first-person plural pronoun according to whether or not the person or persons addressed are associated with the speaker's action. Since, besides the plural, Nama has a dual number and also a masculine, a feminine and an indefinite, common or neuter gender, the pronoun "we" may be translated by ten expressions, each having its special meaning: I and you (masc., sing.) I and he; I and you (fem. sing.) I and she; I and you (masc. pl.) I and you (fem. pl.) I and they (fem. pl.) I and you (com. pl.) I and they (neuter). Thus "the phrase, *we gave to them* may be translated in sixty different ways according to the choice of pronouns." Thus the use of Nama obliges the speaker to indicate details which are of course expressible in European languages by periphrases, but which are not necessarily expressed.

Certain of these differences in meaning are marked in Bantu languages by tone, which is not a lexically significant feature in European languages. In languages which distinguish three tones, what to a European seems like the same syllable may have three different meanings according to whether it is pronounced with a high, middle or low tone. Curiously enough, this important feature of many African languages has often been ignored by amateur linguists who collected word lists or even wrote grammars.

The necessity for communication between groups speaking different languages or dialects gave rise to linguae francae. These are not artificial languages, but languages belonging to certain groups and adopted by other groups as supplementary languages. Thus Swahili, a Bantu language belonging to the people of the Indian Ocean coast, starting from the ports of what is now Tanzania, has spread over the whole eastern part of Africa, through the medium of Arab and African traders. This Swahili lingua franca, which has adopted Arab and English words, has a very poor vocabulary, limited to what is necessary for commercial transactions, and a rudimentary grammar. (It coexists, of course, alongside the full Swahili language which has been discussed above.) In West Africa, Hausa and Fulani have played a similar role. In contemporary Africa, English and French are not only languages of administration and higher education in the new nations, but also the languages for social intercourse between the different language groups who live within the boundaries of a new nation.

The Races of Africa South of the Sahara

Race is not a cultural phenomenon and in itself has no bearing on the social level. It is not because a human group belongs to a certain race that its technology is agricultural rather than industrial, that its political organization is authoritarian rather than democratic, that its art is expressionist rather than realist. Race and culture are two independent variables. However, we treat a race in connection with civilizations because confusion between these two sets of phenomena has prevailed for so long in African studies. As late as 1930, C. G. Seligman had no hesitation in basing his classification of the races of Africa on non-physical criteria such as linguistic family or nomadism.

According to Henri-V. Vallois's definition, races are "natural groups of human beings who have in common a complex of hereditary physical characteristics." The main physical criteria by which races have traditionally been distinguished are skin color, hair type, stature, the shape of the head, face, nose and eyes, and the proportions of blood groups in the population. The last characteristic, whose inheritance pattern is better known than that of the others, unfortunately does not always give results which fit with those based on the former. This shows that the traditional classifications, most of which give four major racial divisions (Khoisan, including Bushmen and Hottentots; Negritos, including Mbuti Pygmies; Negroes, including most of the dark-skinned peoples occupying most of sub-Saharan Africa; and Ethiopians, including the varied populations of north-east Africa) cannot be regarded as definitive, and attempts to revise and refine them are futile unless the assumptions on which they are based are critically examined.

Jean Hiernaux has tried to form new racial classifications by using methods analogous to those by which Greenberg tries to ascertain the common origin of groups of languages. He compares populations with regard to a large number of hereditary characteristics, including many measurements of the body and head, blood groups and fingerprint patterns. A grouping based on any one, or even several of these characteristics would not be significant, for, as with linguistic items, similarities and differences may be due to chance or to recent migrations. But when a large number and variety of characteristics is used as a basis for comparison, regular patterns appear which may be regarded as valid evidence that resemblances between populations indicate a common origin.

The task of the physical anthropologist is complicated by the nature of heredity. The phenotype (the measurable characteristics) of an individual or a group does not always correspond exactly with the genotype (the gene pattern regulating the measurable characteristics). Blood groups represent a good match between phenotype and genotype, but characteristics such as skin color and body build are inherited by mechanisms not fully understood. Some characteristics often used for racial classification, such as nose width and prognathism are not independent variables, but are partly functions of the same hereditary mechanism. All hereditary features are affected by genetic drift (the random redistribution of genetic material from one generation to the next). Many, such as body build, are affected by natural selection (differential adaptation to environment). Recent research suggests that even blood groups are subject to natural selection in that certain blood types are connected with greater or lesser resistance to certain endemic or epidemic diseases. Some measurements, such as stature, are strongly affected by cultural factors such as nutrition.

However, when comparisons are based on a very large number of hereditary features, the statistical probability that similarities and differences in phenotype will truly reflect corresponding similarities and differences in genotype, is high.

So Hiernaux, using a large number of hereditary features, compares 101 African populations in pairs, and calculates the degree of difference between the members of each pair. He then compares each pair with a third population, and the resulting pair with a fourth until all the populations have been compared with each other. He then places all the populations on a two-dimensional diagram which shows the degree of difference between each population and each of the others. If the traditional racial classifications had been valid, the populations so plotted would have formed "constellations" corresponding to "races." Hiernaux found, on the contrary, that his master diagram "showed a cloud of dots spread almost uniformly."

However, this does not mean that all attempts at classification must be abandoned. When the average distance of each population from all the others is worked out and plotted on a diagram, it is found that some populations with a high average distance are on the periphery of the diagram, while others with a low average distance are in the center. Those on the periphery include the Mbuti Pygmies of the Ituri forest in the Congo; the Nuer, who live in the southern Sudan; and the Bisharin, who live on the Red Sea coast. Hiernaux thinks that the high degree of distance of these peoples from the other populations may be due to a combination of one or more of the following factors: genetic drift, natural selection, genetic isolation (especially in the case of the Pygmies); adaptation to a specially harsh environment (especially applicable to the Nuer) or a large degree of genetic influence from outside Africa (applicable to the Bisharin).

The populations with the lowest average distance from all other populations are the Logo (northern Uganda), the Nyamwezi (Great Lakes region), the Dyola (coast of Senegal), the Nyoro (Uganda). Theoretically their low average distance may be due to membership of the main stock from which most of the sub-Saharan Africans descended, adaptation to an intermediate environment, or the product of genetic mixture due to extensive migration. Because most of these peoples live, or have lived until recently, in the savanna areas, and because there is no evidence of genetic mixture between contrasted stocks in them, Hiernaux thinks they may be descended from a major stock which originated in the savanna area of West Africa. From this point of view, the Mbuti Pygmies of the Congo forests may represent an extreme differentiation of such a stock in response to the severe conditions of the rain forest, while the Nuer represent another extreme adaptation to their marshy semidesert.

Although language and race are independent variables, it usually happens that peoples who migrate retain both their language and their unity as an intermarrying population. Thus linguistics and genetics can often be used in conjunction to establish historical reconstructions of major migrations of African populations. Hiernaux conjectures that: "from a comparatively uniform area, a population spread in recent times and occupied a vast area with speakers of Bantu languages all closely related. This linguistic closeness is associated with biological similarities among a series of populations which have remained in much the same environment and have not interbred to any great degree with physically dissimilar populations. Beyond the circle in which these populations live, the Bantu language area is occupied by ethnic groups which differ from the former groups in the smaller part played by the original stock in their genetic make-up and in the effects of a different environment on their physical characteristics."

Hiernaux considers that our present data and techniques do not enable us to say much more than this about the "races" of Africa. The great gaps in our knowledge of the peopling of Africa will only gradually, if ever, be filled in by careful coordination of reliable data supplied by linguists, physical anthropologists, archaeologists and historians.

This kind of collaboration has already made it clear that the distribution of physical types in Africa today is the result of innumerable migrations; the "races" of the modern world cannot in any way be linked to the various types of early man which evolved in Africa during the Pleistocene period: Carleton Coon's attempt to establish such links has been rejected by all other physical anthropologists. *Homo sapiens* is a single species; Dobzhansky writes: "The possibility that the genetic system of living men, *Homo sapiens*, could have independently arisen five times, or even twice, is vanishingly small. A biological species can be likened to a cable consisting of many strands; the strands —populations, tribes and races—may in the course of time subdivide, branch or fuse; some of them may fade away and others may become more vigorous and multiply. It is, however, the whole species that is eventually transformed into a new species. Adaptively valuable gene patterns arise in different populations of the species. The populations, or races, in which these evolutionary inventions have occurred then increase in number, spread, come in contact with other populations, hybridize with them, form superior new gene patterns that spread from new centers and thus continue the process of change." This, in general terms, is the history of the races of Africa.

Another human characteristic that emerges when the work of physical anthropologists, linguists, archaeologists and historians is put together is man's capacity for rapid change, both physical and cultural. The complexities of the physical and cultural history of man in Africa—or, indeed, anywhere in the world—make it impossible to link any cultural achievement with any physical characteristic, and thus cultural advances cannot be attributed to racial superiority.

Meanwhile it is of some value to indicate briefly the main categories of physical types in Africa, based on the traditional anthropometric and somatological criteria.

This information, which is still fragmentary, has been put together by Vallois. The northern Sahara is occupied by white races. In the south, Vallois distinguishes four races very unequal in the numbers of their members: the Khoisans, the Negritos, the Ethopians and the Negroes.

The Hottentots and the Bushmen are the only contemporary representatives of the Khoisan race, the word Khoisan being composed of the term *Khoi* by which the Hottentots designate themselves, and the term *san*, their name for the Bushmen. This race, which is dying out, is similar to the Negritos in one respect, that of stature. Nearly all the Negritos are less than five feet tall (measurements taken of the Mbuti Pygmies show an average height for men of four feet eight inches). The Bushmen are somewhat taller, but still short, about five feet two inches on the average. For the southern Bushmen, probably the least mixed, the average goes down to four feet six or seven inches. But in features other than height there are very marked differences.

The Negritos have a yellowish-brown skin, kinky hair and abundant body hair. They are slightly dolichocephalic; seen from above their heads are only a little longer from back to front than from side to side. Their lips are thick but not everted, their noses very broad in proportion to the length. They have stocky bodies and short limbs. The proportion of their blood groups is different from that of other African populations: group O is less frequent, while there is a high proportion of groups B and AB.

The Bushmen have a light skin, varying from pale yellow to yellowish-brown; being very dry and deeply wrinkled, it looks too large for the body. There is almost no body hair, the bone structure is light, the joints very delicate, hands and feet very small. The buttocks appear very prominent because of a deep lumber curvature of the spine and because of steatopygia, which is very marked in the women. The Bushmen have broad, flat faces, jutting cheekbones, receding chins, noneverted lips, lobe-less ears, narrow, slightly slanting eye openings, but without the Mongolian epicanthal fold. Their short, fine black hair grows in little separate tufts; this type of hair is called peppercorn hair.

The Ethiopian race occupies the easternmost region of Africa, the Eastern Horn. They are moderately dolichocephalic and their average height is five feet five inches. Their skin color varies from reddish-brown to blackish-brown. They have little body hair, and their hair is curly or wavy but not kinky. Their lips are thin and not everted, their noses jutting and not flattened.

These characteristics, which are intermediate between those of the Blacks and the Whites, have been considered as the result of interbreeding. However, Vallois regards the Ethopians rather as "a primary stock which has not become clearly differentiated either in the White or the Black direction. This would explain why the usual Ethopian type is so different from that of mulattoes. Interbreeding would have occurred only at a later stage." Such interbreeding is thought to have given rise to the Massai, Nandi and Suk groups to the south of the Abyssianian block, and to the Fulani to the west.

By far the most numerous is the Negro race: it is found all over Africa south of the Sahara and west of the Eastern Horn; it is the race typical of Black Africa, the race to which we refer when we speak of the Black or Negro race. Its most obvious characteristic is the skin color which varies from light brown to black. This deep pigmentation absorbs heat, which is not an advantage in hot countries, but intercepts the ultra-violet rays, which prevents sunstroke. Vallois also states that resistance to high temperatures is due to the large number of sweat glands which secrete twice as much perspiration as those of Europeans. There is almost no body hair; the hair is very short and kinky. Stature varies, but is usually above five feet eight inches. The head is usually dolichocephalic. The face has prominent cheekbones and always shows a certain degree of prognathism; the nose is broad and the nostrils extend into horizontal slits; the lips are thick with part of the red rim everted. The hips are narrow and the shoulders broad.

Within this broad racial group, "although the present state of our knowledge precludes the establishment of definitive categories," Vallois distinguishes "provisionally" five sub-races based on anthropometric measurements. These are: the Sudanese sub-race, situated in the savanna zone which extends between the equatorial forest and the Sahara, from Senegal to Kordofan; the Guinean sub-race, in the forest strip which extends along the gulf coast from Guinea to Cameroon; the Congolese sub-race in the equatorial forest and the savanna zone south of it; the Nilotic sub-race in the marshes and steppes of the Nile from Khartoum to Lake Victoria; the South African or Zambezian sub-race in the eastern half of the continent from the Great Lakes to the southern tip.

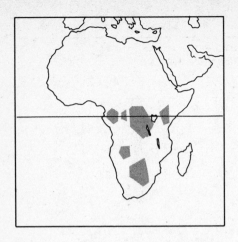

THE CIVILIZATION
OF THE BOW

The Art of the Hunters

Thousands of rock paintings have been discovered in the southern part of Africa, extending from the eighth parallel to the Cape. Paintings and engravings are especially numerous in the Republic of South Africa, on both slopes of the Drakensberg chain. (See map below.) They show that the painters and gravers were fully masters of their techniques. This is astonishing, for these artists belong to the most materially impoverished peoples who have ever existed. The entire possessions of a man or a woman are limited to what can be carried in a small bag; they build no permanent dwellings; they lead a hard, perilous life, which must have given rise to constant anxieties. Yet they create works of beauty.

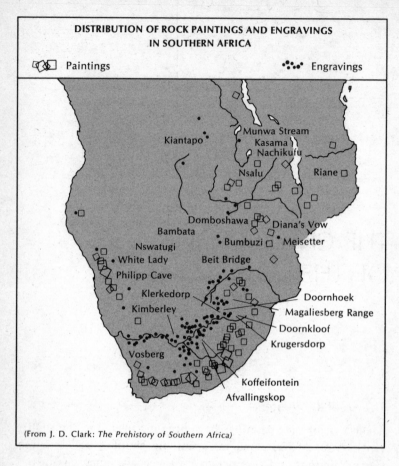

DISTRIBUTION OF ROCK PAINTINGS AND ENGRAVINGS IN SOUTHERN AFRICA

Paintings   Engravings

Kiantapo

Munwa Stream
Kasama
Nachikufu

Nsalu

Riane

Domboshawa
Bambata

Diana's Vow

Bumbuzi   Meisetter

Nswatugi
White Lady
Philipp Cave

Beit Bridge

Klerkedorp

Doornhoek
Magaliesberg Range

Kimberley

Doornkloof
Krugersdorp

Vosberg

Koffeifontein
Afvallingskop

(From J. D. Clark: *The Prehistory of Southern Africa*)

They are drawn on sheltered rocks. In the Natal area especially these shelters are on the dry, sunny side of a mountain, not far from water supplies; they command a broad view. These places, which were mostly inhabited, receive natural light; in this they differ from the dark caves in Europe where certain prehistoric wall paintings are found. The engravings were made by two different methods; by a linear incision cutting through the patina caused by exposure to the atmosphere, to the deep color of the rock; and by punching, marking the outlines of the design,

and even some surfaces, by small holes. The tool used for incision, which must have been a sort of stone chisel, has not yet
been found, but we possess some of the pointed stones which
could have been used for punching. The colors used in the paintings are reds, yellows, oranges, grayish-blues, and also black
and white. How were these colors obtained? Mineral oxides
supplied the pigments: iron oxide heated to various temperatures gives several shades of red, yellow and black, hematite
gives red and limonite yellow. Black is also obtained from
charcoal, white from kaolin, bird droppings or euphorbia sap.
These pigments were ground to powder which was then mixed
with animal fat (the marrow of the eland was often used), the
sap of certain plants, milk, blood or urine. These mixtures held
together perfectly, and in certain cases we can tell that the
colors have hardly deteriorated, even when they were exposed
to frequent rains. In certain soft rocks the colors penetrated
deeply. The paint was applied by various instruments which
could be used as fine paint-brushes, brushes, styluses, or knives:
gnu-tail hair, feathers, flexible bones, pointed sticks and, of
course, human fingers.

Two traditions appear very clearly in this rock art: representational and abstract. The abstract is represented by far fewer
works, concentrated in the region west of the Kafue and north
of the Zambezi. Thus in Katanga we find geometrical forms,
chevrons, checkerboard patterns, herringbones; in Angola, con-
centric circles and other curved lines; in Zambia, parallel lines
and inverted U's with a straight line across the middle, etc. These
go beyond mere decoration and come into the domain of signs,
stylized drawings which evoke actual beings or ideas. The representational tradition is much more important and is preponderant
over all of southern Africa in the number and quality of the
pictures. This is the kind of art which astounded Westerners
because it is so unlike our naïve conception of "primitive" art:
we expect childish drawings in which the artist has clumsily
tried to reproduce some mental image (a man is a rectangle with

two lines below, a line on each side and a circle on top) rather than a visual image. On the contrary, the rock painters of southern Africa reproduce what they see very skillfully. They depict animals not only in profile but in difficult attitudes, turning around, for example, or in rapid movement. They use shading to pass from one color to another and also to give an impression of depth. However, they seem to concentrate their attention on the individual animal. When a herd is represented, the animals are juxtaposed, rather than arranged in depth, so that the more distant ones are partly masked by the nearer ones.

These qualities may be seen when the subjects represented are animals. For humans, the method is different. Movement is always depicted just as intensely, but the individual is usually drawn as a monochrome silhouette. These silhouettes are very expressive; accentuating some features and minimizing others, they succeed in characterizing their subjects very clearly. These interpretations retain their liveliness and do not seem to have become stereotyped: there are women with huge breasts and others with very small breasts, hunters with exaggeratedly developed calves and others with almost stick-like legs.

We have already mentioned some of the chief subjects of these paintings and engravings; large animals, buffalo, eland, antelopes, lions, etc., which until a hundred years ago were so common in the wooded savannas of southern Africa. Then came isolated human beings, among whom may be distinguished individuals belonging to different populations characterized by certain physical features, such as steatopygia (fat buttocks) or ornaments such as arm or leg bracelets, or objects such as musical instruments or shields; some of these human beings are European men and women, soldiers and horsemen. Last and most important are hunting scenes, ceremonies, dances, cattle-raiding expeditions, battles. Who are the artists who created these works, some of which are of superb quality? Where did they learn their craft? To what periods do they go back? Such questions have been posed since the eighteenth century. They are still far from being answered. However, as long ago as 1721, the Bishop of Mozambique informed the Lisbon Royal Academy of History of the existence of rock paintings in that territory, and since Johannes Schumacher in 1776 made the first copies of the paintings discovered north of the Cape, not a few mysteries have been cleared up and some important pieces of information have become known.

These paintings represent a tradition which has remained alive from prehistoric times to the nineteenth century, which is a very rare phenomenon in cultural evolution. And they bring us into immediate contact with a way of life which was certainly the earliest human civilization, that of the hunters, the ancestors of all men who live on the earth today. To place in context the tradition of African rock painting we must step back for a moment, and go a long way back into the past.

Africa, Cradle of Humanity

In the present state of our knowledge, it appears that there is some truth behind the expression "man was born in Africa." It is thought that the earliest forms of near-man and true man evolved in the savanna areas of eastern and southern Africa.

Modern man (*Homo sapiens*) and the great apes do not belong to the same evolutionary line. Man and apes do, of course, have a common ancestor, but the evolutionary lines of man and of the apes diverged several—perhaps between 10 and 30—million years ago. Paleontologists have made considerable progress in discovering the various forms that led up to modern man. Some distinguish four main stages in the evolution of man: the Australopithecines, the Pithecanthropines, the Neanderthals and modern man. Others, however, including some of the most eminent and respected anthropologists have other views: some think that some or all of the Australopithecines are not directly ancestral to modern man, but are a side branch from the main line of human evolution: some do not regard the Neanderthals as a separate species but as a minor variation of the types leading by gradual stages to modern man. It is impossible to summarize here the many views about the creatures which led to modern man. I can only outline what is generally agreed on by the major paleontologists, archaeologists and physical anthropologists.

About two million years ago, perhaps earlier, several varieties of creatures known as the Australopithecines ranged over much of central, eastern and southern Africa, where the natural vegetation was mainly savanna. There are several varieties of the Australopithecines, and we do not yet know their exact genetic relationship; some authorities think that the smaller forms were earlier than the later, while others think that several varieties existed at the same time. Some of the Australopithecines were much smaller than modern man, being about four feet tall and weighing about fifty to eighty pounds. Their cranial capacity, which indicates the size of the brain, was about 500 cc., which is about the same as that of the modern chimpanzee (but brain-size is not a good indicator of mental capacity), and the shape of the skull and face was more ape-like than man-like. However, they had other features which were very human. Their teeth resembled those of modern man. They walked fully erect, for the shape of the pelvis is adapted for erect posture, and the foramen magnum, the hole through which the spinal cord comes up into the cranium, is at the bottom of the skull rather than the back, showing that the Australopithecines held the head erect. The most famous of the near-men of this time is *Homo habilis* discovered by Leakey in Bed I of Olduvai Gorge located in Tanzania and so named because Leakey thinks that he made the "tools" found with his remains. Other anthropologists, however, think that these "tools" were not manufactured at all but were merely natural pebbles, and still others believe that even if they were real tools they were not necessarily made by *Homo habilis* but could have been made by other forms of near-man or early man found in nearby sites.

Another variety of the Australopithecines, *Australopithecus robustus,* formerly called Paranthopus, is rather larger than the other types and is thought by some anthropologists to be a little more recent. It is about the size of modern man; it is also more man-like than the other Australopithecines in its dentition: its canine teeth are proportionately smaller and its molars larger.

One of the Australopithecines which has captured the popular imagination, Zinjanthropus, was also discovered by Leakey. He gave it a name of its own, *Zinjanthropus boisei,* but most anthropologists regard it as one of the Australopithecines, probably a larger and earlier variety.

All further statements that could be made about the Australopithecines would be highly controversial; we do not yet know (the vast amount of literature contains more speculation than evidence) whether or not they made or used tools, whether they were direct ancestors of modern man or a collateral branch which was superseded by a better adapted type.

The controversies about whether or not the Australopithecines made tools and about whether the so-called Kafuan tools are tools at all, are especially lively because many anthropologists and philosophers regard tool-making as the most important archaeologically observable feature distinguishing man from nonhuman animals. (Language would, of course, be a better criterion, but we have no means of knowing at what point in human evolution the capacity for language occurred. The whole question of the relationship between language capacity and observable anatomical characteristics of the brain-case, mouth and other parts of the body concerned with speech is another highly controversial area of physical anthropology.) A definition of man is one of those undertakings in which philosophers have never been able to achieve success. Many prehistorians and anthropologists define man as a tool-making animal. Other animals sometimes use tools, but to create them presupposes a degree of mental development which is regarded as human. (Some anthropologists and naturalists, however, report instances of tool-making by nonhuman animals.) Of course there are other activities peculiar to human beings, but I prefer the criterion of tool-making because it has left material evidence which prehistorians can discover. And it has the merit not only of convenience, but it serves as a universal constant for all cultures: the conquest of nature by man. The making of a crude stone hand-axe is a first, big step in the direction of man's mastery over nature.

If, then, it could be shown that Zinjanthropus or any of the other Australopithecines or *Homo habilis* really made tools, it would mean that a creature differing considerably in anatomy, especially in brain size, from modern man, was capable of an important human activity. This would be of great importance to both anthropologists and philosophers. Unfortunately the question must await further archaeological and paleontological evidence.

A creature much more similar to modern man, Pithecanthropus or *Homo erectus*, was first discovered in Java. Similar remains were found in Choukoutien, China, where they were associated with fire and tools, some of which suggested that animals were killed for both food and skins. The cranial capacity of Pithecanthropus was about 1000 cc., about the lower limit of the range for modern man, and its pelvis was adapted for erect walking. Its dentition suggests that its diet included meat.

Pithecanthropus types were found in Africa by Leakey in Bed II of Olduvai Gorge, i.e. in the stratum above and thus more recent than Bed I, where the Australopithecines were found. The African Pithecanthropines lived about half a million years ago, about the same time as their counterparts in China. They do not seem to have used fire, but they did make tools.

It seems that the Pithecanthropines were much more widely distributed than the previous forms of near-man. Anthropologists disagree about the significance of this; present evidence is insufficient to indicate whether the Pithecanthropines evolved in one location and then dispersed, or whether parallel evolution occurred in Africa and Asia. They also disagree about the relationship between the Australopithecines, the Pithecanthropines and modern man: there may have been one, two or three evolutionary lines.

Remains of early man were found in 1921 at Broken Hill in Zambia and in 1953 at Sadanha on the south-west coast of South Africa. These types, sometimes called *Homo rhodesiensis*, lived about 40,000 or 50,000 years ago. They are sometimes classified with the Neanderthal types found in Europe and Asia, which were associated with the Mousterian culture of stone tools. However, some anthropologists do not accept this classification, and others do not regard the Neanderthals as a separate type at all, but rather a variety of *Homo sapiens* or modern man. In any case, these early men resemble the "Neanderthals" in that they have heavy brow ridges and large teeth, but in stature, brain size and erect posture they are like modern man. They made stone tools of the types known as Sangoan and Fauresmithian. Sangoan tools include picks which could be used for digging roots; they are found in forest regions. The Fauresmithian tools are more adapted to the drier savanna regions in which they were found; they consist mainly of handaxes and cleavers.

The evolutionary relationship of the Rhodesian types to modern man is still controversial.

The first use of fire in Africa (it seems to have been used earlier in Asia) was about 50,000 or 60,000 years ago. This, together with the development of a more efficient and varied tool-kit, seems to have enabled human populations to spread over the whole of southern Africa during this period, which is known as the Middle Pleistocene. (The terminology for the geological and cultural period of Africa has not yet been adequately correlated with that for European geology, paleontology and archaeology.)

By the time of the Upper Pleistocene, about 33,000 to 10,000 years ago, cultures popularly known as the Middle Stone Age cultures were flourishing in sub-Saharan Africa. There was now much more regional variation in tool types, though most were based on the technique of the prepared core and faceted flake. "Thus we find the Stillbay and Pietersburg variants in the savannah and grasslands of south and east Africa concentrating on light cutting, piercing and projectile tools of stone, while in the Congo forests, for example, the contemporary form, known as Lupemban, contains many axe and chopping elements and magnificent lanceolate knives or stabbing points." (J. Desmond Clark)

Together with the Middle Stone Age tool traditions appears evidence of religious and aesthetic behavior, manifested not only in the increased sense of style shown in the tools but also in careful burial of the dead and in the use of paint and ornamentation.

About the end of the Pleistocene (8000 B.C. plus or minus 2000 years) migration into and within Africa, together with a change to a rather wetter climate, brought still further variety into the tools and cultures of sub-Saharan Africa. New fishing techniques permitted permanent settlements to be established on rivers, lakes and seashores. This period is called by Desmond Clark the Post-Pleistocene Stone Age or Later Stone Age. Tools were even more varied, and included microlithic tools, end-scrapers, and devices such as the bow and arrow, poison and barbed fish spears, which enabled their users to obtain more meat and fish for their diet. "These contacts (migration from north and north-east Africa) resulted, for example, in the Congo with the final Middle Stone Age, in the appearance of tanged projectile heads, and in South Africa and Rhodesia in the appearance of new forms of tools made on blades. Similarly, the bifacial foliate points of the later Aterian, the transverse arrowheads and heavy lunate forms of the Mesolithic, and the bifaced axe element of the Neolithic are probably the result of diffusion northwards from the Lupemban and Tshitolian of Equatoria." (J. Desmond Clark)

Clark thinks it possible that some of the stone industries of the Later Stone Age can be associated with the ancestors of modern populations of certain parts of Africa. "In South Africa the Smithfield of the high veld, using various forms of end-scrapers made from indurated shale, is very different from the crescent-like microliths of the Wilton culture, though both were made by

Bushmen and both had a number of traits in common." It is at this point, then, that we can look for some continuity between the prehistoric cultures of Africa and the most archaic of the contemporary cultures, those of the Bushmen and the Pygmies. But although we can speak of continuity in a general sense, we have no knowledge of the exact nature and interrelationship of the many kinds of human culture which must have existed in sub-Saharan Africa between the time of the earliest men and that of the modern Bushmen. We cannot even rely on ancient tools and human remains to tell us at what point in his biological and cultural evolution man became a hunter.

The archaeological and experimental work of George B. Schaller and Gordon R. Lowther shows that it was possible for man to have made meat an important part of his diet before the invention of projectile weapons, and to achieve quite a complex social organization—and cooperative hunting is possible with quite a simple form of social organization—before the beginning of language. Schaller and Lowther think it very unlikely that man in his present form ever lived on a completely vegetarian diet. Early man may have obtained some of his meat, even before he became a skilled hunter, by some scavenging and by killing newly born or sick animals, by running animals down or by eating ones which had recently died of natural causes. He may also have driven larger animals over cliffs or into swamps and then killed and butchered them. It is probable that early man, like some modern hunters and gatherers, enjoyed a mixed diet in which meat was the most valued element, though not usually the largest.

I have given a very brief account of the main lines of African prehistory, because the Late Stone Age is not yet over for a few small groups of men, the Bushman hunters and the Pygmies. But before turning to them I shall try to place rock painting in the succession of prehistoric cultures.

First of all, we know that rock painting was still practised quite recently. In 1869 one of the last Bushman painters was still alive. Also, certain subjects must have been painted after recent events, such as the arrival of the Europeans. But this does not mean that all the paintings were done by the Bushmen during the two last centuries. After an intense study over six years, Abbé Henri Breuil estimates that some of these works are very old. He bases his opinion mostly on the subjects represented, in which he believes he can recognize characters from the civilizations of classical antiquity. Thus in his study devoted to the White Lady of Brandberg (in Southwest Africa), he sees in this fine painting reminiscences of Cretan representations of women bullfighters at Knossos. These influences he claims could have made themselves felt by way of the Egypt of the Pharaohs. He also sees in the procession which accompanies the White Lady certain suggestions of the resurrection myths of Isis, Osiris and Horus. In certain paintings, musical instruments which might be Greek, and rectangular quivers which might be Sumerian, have been pointed out. Certainly such influences are not impossible, but to the present we have no evidence other than a certain interpretation of the pictures, which may not be the only one possible. White is a ritual color among many Bantu peoples, and the various "foreign" objects could well belong to local cultures. Also, until there is proof to the contrary, one may doubt that the rock painting of southern Africa has been exposed to Mediterranean influence and could therefore be dated indirectly through the representation of Cretan or Ancient Egyptian subjects.

There are much clearer similarities between the rock paintings of southern Africa and those of the Sahara and Spain. Must we then conclude that at a certain time a single culture extended from Spain to the Cape? It is one hypothesis, but one which must not exclude the possible explanation of parallel invention. It is not surprising that groups of hunters, confronted with similar problems, might resolve them in a very similar manner and that in this way their cultures would show resemblances even in artistic expression.

We cannot use stratigraphic methods to date these paintings precisely. They are often superimposed one upon the other, but attempts to find a correspondence between these layers and the succession of prehistoric industries have not produced any certain results. The animals represented cannot teach us much about the age of the rock paintings, since the fauna has remained essentially the same since the Upper Pleistocene. The way in which the paint is patinated on the rock gives us few indications, because we do not know much about the characteristics of aging of different types of rock. It seems, however, that granites peel off and sandstones crumble at such a rate that the paintings could not go back thousands of years. In conclusion, we agree with the careful and conservative opinion of J. Desmond Clark on this difficult question of the age of rock paintings. He estimates that with the exception of certain engravings it is very unlikely that the works we possess today go back beyond the Christian era at the earliest, but they probably belong to a tradition of painting which may go back to the beginning of the Late Stone Age (about 5500 B.C.). In fact, if rock painting had not begun earlier than the time of the examples we know, it would have suddenly achieved a very high degree of perfection without any tentative beginnings, which would certainly be very extraordinary.

Pygmies and Bushmen

Rock paintings and engravings do not tell us everything about the life of Late Stone Age hunters. But by filling out the picture they give us with the ethnographic observation that it was possible to carry out among the last bands of hunters before their extinction, we can obtain an idea of this culture.

Life without agriculture or husbandry, of course except under very special conditions, does not enable one to enjoy a certain and abundant food supply. It is, however, a way of life which has enabled African populations to subsist for the last seven or eight thousand years, even if we consider here only the populations with the equipment of the Late Stone Age, without going back to *Zinjanthropus* and his descendants who survived more than a million years with a mental potential and a tool-kit incomparably more rudimentary.

However, this way of life is doomed in modern Africa, and therefore the groups which still practice it are very small and are no longer able to live a full life. They have been pushed back by newcomers with more effective techniques of production into the most inhospitable areas: deserts and the deep forest. How can hunters go on living in the Kalahari Desert, where game is scarce because there is so little water and vegetation? The hunters' retreat began under pressure from farmers, long before the arrival of the Europeans, but it was accelerated, especially in South Africa, where, about 1890, the last bands of Bushmen living in the still game-rich regions of the Drakensberg, in Natal, were exterminated. At the present time most hunting groups in Africa have become marginal peoples. The way of life of this "Lumpenproletariat" would not deserve to be classed in the rank of the great African civilizations if we did not consider it in its historical and prehistorical perspective. The only reason we deal with the Bushmen and Pygmies of the present day is that they give us information about the hunters of the past who had elaborated a system of collective living which enabled innumerable generations to subsist and even to carry on a fully human life.

It is not usual to treat the Pygmies and the Bushmen together. In fact they are often contrasted, thus giving more importance to race than to culture. For, though they have the same way of life in the most essential features, techniques and economy, Pygmies and Bushmen belong to different stocks. But since they have found the same solution to the basic problem of subsistence, they belong to the same civilization, based on direct taking of the materials offered by the habitat.

Gathering

These materials are obtained not only by hunting, but just as importantly by gathering. The latter activity is usually performed by women, while hunting is an occupation reserved for men. This division of labor is self-explanatory: hunting requires qualities which women, subject to the demands of maternity, develop to a lesser degree than men. However this does not result —as happens in other cultures—in a sexual division of labor so rigid that feminine tasks are forbidden to men for reasons of religion, prestige or dignity. The Mbuti hunter of the Ituri does not mind picking up on the way home from his hunting expeditions the innumerable species of mushrooms that abound in the forest; similarly, he does not look down on giving his wife a hand when she has discovered a particularly large colony of caterpillars. And on the other hand though women and children usually do the gathering they are of great help in the task of beating game towards the nets in the course of a drive. In the activities of women and children are included the catching of small animals, insects, reptiles, crayfish, moles, and fieldmice. Men and women alike gather termites.

The forest hunters live in the vast, dense lush world of the equatorial region. In the deep shade of the giant trees, the vegetation which grows in layer upon layer offers them an environment in which conditions of life are harsh. According to Paul Schebesta's description, the torrential rains which pour down the year round with little variation combine with the extreme heat to produce a constant hothouse atmosphere. "Every morning thick mists rise from the saturated earth, and the thickets remain soaking wet for hours." When the sun breaks through, the Mbuti women go out in single file to visit parts of the forest they have previously marked out, avoiding the dense islands of brush where game takes shelter. They pile into their baskets, held on their backs by a tump line, all the edible products they can find according to the season. The forest is generous in berries and wild fruits, juicy green leaves and stems, and nourishing roots. With a knife, which they always carry stuck into their belts, they cut and peel young branches to extract the edible pith. They use a pointed stick to dig up tubers and the bulbs of certain plants. They heap small animals, crabs, crayfish and snails, which they gather in the streams, into leaves folded into a cone.

In the wooded savanna of Lesotho and the mountains of the Drakensberg, where the Bushman hunters lived before taking refuge in the Kalahari Desert, nature is certainly less luxurious, but it still offers a great variety of products: berries, wild melons, baobab fruits. There could be found in abundance small bulbs which could be eaten raw or peeled and cooked under the ashes. The women also gathered the seeds of various grasses which they ground to flour in mortars hollowed out of the rock. There was also a variety of small animals which could be caught or gathered: reptiles, tortoises, lizards, monitor lizards, not counting the various kinds of eggs, of which the most appreciated is the ostrich egg.

The Kalahari is so poor a habitat that food-gathering is an arduous enterprise. However, it is there that the last bands of Bushman hunters were pushed back till they could go no further under the pressure of Black farmers and herdsmen and European settlers. The most important part of the food-gathering by women consists of insects, grasshoppers or termites.

Termite hills are also greatly sought after by the hunters of the equatorial forest. The systematic manner in which they are utilized helps us to understand that gathering is not, as one might think, a haphazard activity; it is nearly always methodical and has a certain kind of periodicity and predictability. According to Schebesta, the termite hills are first located and ownership marked by trampling the earth around them. The women visit them often, so as not to miss the swarming, which is the best time for the harvest. They scrape away the thin layer of earth and expose the corridors of the termite hill; small bits of wood are stuck into the openings; they are removed from time to time to watch for the moment when the termites are about to come to the surface: this means that they are about to swarm. The man who has taken possession of the termite hill goes and settles there with his family, and builds a shelter. Termites begin to swarm at twilight. A fire burns under a roof of leaves in front of a ditch dug at the foot of the termite hill. The termites as they take flight bump into the roof, fall to the ground, turn towards the bright firelight, and fall into the ditch, which is soon full of insects; the Pygmy woman picks them up with a shovel and puts them into a basket which she covers with leaves; in this way the harvest is brought back to camp.

Thus gathering is not a simple activity; it requires a certain organization, the use of techniques, a scientific knowledge of the flora and fauna of the area, so as to avoid poisonous species and get the best out of the edible ones. And when one realizes how simple is these peoples' tool-kit one understands that they have had to use their great ingenuity to subsist in the extreme ecological conditions to which they have recently been confined. Actually, the Bushman woman's only tool is a digging-stick, which, however, is much more perfected than that of the Ituri woman. It is a staff about as long as its user is tall, an antelope horn is attached to the digging end, and it is weighted in the middle by a pierced stone. This addition gives more weight to the stick so that it can be used in the hard earth of the Kalahari. When the stick was worn out or broken, the stone was carefully kept, for it took about ten days to make a hole in a stone by means of an instrument made of lydite, a very hard black stone.

Wild bees produce a honey which all hunting peoples gather. This is very difficult when, as in the Drakensberg, the hives must first be located in the crevices of a cliff, and then the honey got out. Towards evening the Bushman would lie in wait for the pollen-laden bees and try to follow them to their home; he was helped in this enterprise by a little bird which, fluttering around the men, led them to the hives, attracted by the honey which it loved and could not get at unaided. When the hive had been found, the honey-gatherer had himself lowered down the cliff face by a strong rope and he built near the hive a wooden platform on which he stood to operate.

Life is difficult enough in the forest and the wooded savanna; but it becomes a series of precarious triumphs in the desert where the Bushmen were obliged to take refuge. Here every search is arduous, even the search for water. Water sources are scarce, and most of the time it is not possible to set up the camp near water, for fear of scaring the game. When water sources are not available, the Bushmen have to resort to complicated procedures. Here is Arnot's description of one of these operations which he witnessed in 1881; we take it from Victor Ellenberger. "Finally our oxen showed their extreme fatigue, and as they were about to collapse we sent them ahead without the waggon. Very fortunately for us a band of wandering Bushmen arrived; at our urgent request and the offer of a good reward, they set to looking here and there to find water. They made their choice at a place where there was growing a sort of plant with a bulbous root; the little men then began to dig in the sand with their hands until they had made in the soft sand a hole nearly nine feet deep in the form of an inverted cone. This done, one of the Bushmen, who appeared to be the expert of the band, took several reeds of different lengths and slid head first to the bottom of the hole. Then he took the first reed, in the end of which was inserted a little grass to make a filter, preventing sand from getting into the reed, and gradually stuck it into the sand, then he added a second reed, sealing the joint with a thin layer of gum. Then, setting his mouth to the end of the second reed, and alternately blowing and sucking the reed, he loked at us over his shoulder with a smile of satisfaction: he had, he said, smelled the taste of water, but we would have to be patient for a while. About six hours later he slid down again into the hole, taking with him this time a tortoise shell: again setting his mouth to the end of the reed he sucked up with each breath a mouthful of water which he emptied into the tortoise shell, squirting it out of the side of his mouth until it was full."

The Bushmen use similar methods to extract water from trees and wild melons. At times of extreme drought they are reduced to extracting from the stomach cavities of animals a greenish juice which can be drunk.

Storing water presents some difficulties for people who do not make pottery. The Bushmen usually use the shells of ostrich eggs, which they bury in the sand. They also use bags made from antelope stomachs.

Hunting in the Desert

In the desert environment of the Kalahari, hunting has become an incredibly difficult activity. As the range of a bowshot is less than fifty yards, the hunter must get very near to the animal in open country, with no high vegetation. He has to use various ruses, such as disguising himself as an ostrich and imitating its gait so as to be able to get very close to a flock of these birds. He may sometimes have to stalk a kudu for several days before he can attack it. This may require a lone hunter to walk a long way, which may take him very far from camp and water holes. When the hunter is at last near enough to the animal to reach it with an arrow, the shot rarely brings a large animal down: the stone point would inflict only a wound which would heal if the arrowhead were not poisoned. But vegetable poison acts slowly. Before finishing off the animal, the hunter may have to follow it perhaps thirty-five to forty miles if it is strong. Certainly the hunter will try to drive the animal towards the camp so as not to have to carry a heavy carcass unaided. On the other hand, he cannot leave it while he goes for help without the risk of finding on his return only the skeleton of the game he has brought down. Although various methods of hunting are practised, the basic weapon used as much by the Pygmies as by the Bushmen, as much in the forest as in the desert, is the bow. But it is not always the same kind of bow. The Mbuti bow is small, rarely longer than a man's arm, while that of the Naron, who are southern Bushmen, is sometimes as long as four and a half feet, but rarely longer. This essential hunting weapon is made with the greatest care. The Mbuti use four kinds of wood. To shape wood for a bow, they have to take a smooth wood, which they first peel, then sand into shape with a grater; it is round and its diameter is about half an inch to an inch. For bowstrings they use only split fibers from certain species of trees or certain stems. The Naron bow is semicircular in section in the middle, and the string is made from animal tendons.

There are many other tools for hunting. Thus a Naron hunter's equipment includes a hook for digging small rodents, lizards and snakes out of their holes, and a staff about four and a half feet long weighted in the same way as the women's digging sticks, which can be used to beat and very rarely throw at an animal. The Naron, like other Bushmen, use traps, which are of the noose or ditch type. The ostrich trap consists of a running knot in which the ostrich, attracted by a melon, gets caught. The Mbuti, on the other hand, refuse to use traps, although they are in contact with peoples who know of them.

These hunters' tool-kits are very rudimentary, since their cultural heritage does not include iron weapons. Of course modern Bushmen and Pygmies use knives and other metal instruments obtained from neighboring farmers or Europeans, but for thousands of years hunting societies have lived entirely without these.

Fire

Although it has never been used to obtain metals, fire has an essential place in their daily life and in their mental world. The Mbuti always keep burning brands in camp and when they move they always carry with them a few burning embers wrapped in leaves. As soon as they halt they relight these embers. This is not because they are incapable of producing fire, but rather because in the extreme humidity of the tropical forest this is a lengthy operation. The Bushmen always carry with them the two small pieces of wood with which they make fire. The method used to make fire is described as follows by an old woman of a neighboring tribe, the Suto, as Ellenberger reports.

"Fire was made with small sticks of different kinds of wood, river willow, for example. . . . The lower stick was laid horizontally on the ground and a little hole was made in it, into which the upper stick, held vertically, would fit; a slit was made at the edge of the hole so that the sparks could spurt out and set fire to the shreds of tinder plant which were arranged around it. These sticks were called male (the upper one) and female (the lower one). To make fire the Bushmen worked in pairs, one holding the female stick down on the ground, the other rubbing, that is, spinning the male stick very fast; soon through the friction, sparks flew out and set fire to the shreds of tinder."

This precious fire, which served to keep people warm (even in the equatorial forest the dampness makes the night seem quite cold), to protect, to reassure, to cook food, was for the hunters much more than a commodity in their hard life; it was their invention, it was what distinguished them from the other inhabitants of the forest or the savanna. According to the myths reported by Schebesta, the Mbuti of the Ituri tell that it was one of them who, long ago, stole fire. According to another legend, it was seized from Mugu, an almighty supernatural being; according to yet another it was stolen from the chimpanzees. The legend involving the chimpanzees follows:

On one of his many journeys, a Mbuti came one day upon a chimpanzee village, whose inhabitants welcomed him warmly. In the evening he crouched with them by the fire, which delighted him with its warmth and dancing flame. At once he got the idea of bringing fire back to his camp. He thought of a trick to steal a brand. From that time the Mbuti was on many occasions a guest in the chimpanzee village. One fine day he arrived wearing a strange loincloth. The grown-up chimpanzees were busy in their gardens and only the chimpanzee children were left; they laughed at the oddly dressed Pygmy. He had fastened to his belt a long train of beaten bark, which hung down to the ground. When he was served the usual bananas, he crouched with them so close to the fire that the bark train was in great danger of catching fire. "Look out, Mbuti, your *murumba* will catch fire!" cried the chimpanzee children. "Doesn't much matter, it is plenty long enough," replied the Pygmy, feigning indifference, and he went on chewing his bananas.

But he was secretly watching his train which gradually began to turn red, until suddenly, taking advantage of an opportunity, he leaped up and sped away. The chimpanzee children, astonished, began to scream at the top of their voices, which brought the old chimpanzees running. They found out what had happened and guessed immediately that the Mbuti had stolen the fire by a trick. They rushed off in pursuit of him, but the Pygmies could run faster than they. When the chimpanzees arrived at the Mbuti camp, fires were burning merrily everywhere. 'Why did you steal fire from us, instead of buying it from us honestly?' they cried to the Pygmies. But the Mbuti refused to be intimidated by their insults, and the chimpanzees returned frustrated to their village. They were so furious with the ingratitude of the Mbuti, who had stolen bananas from them (this is told in another legend), that they abandoned their village and retreated to the forest, where they live without either fire or bananas, and have as their only food wild fruits.

Another tale associates the theft of fire with Tore, a supernatural being, and with the coming of death to men. A Mbuti stole fire from Tore's old mother and she died of cold. Tore, unable to catch the thief, proclaimed him his own equal, but added that men should also die, as a punishment.

Forest Hunting

Individual hunting is practised in the savannas and the deserts, but rarely in the forest. There, hunting usually takes the form of a short tracking expedition. Several hunters armed with bows and arrows follow the hunt leader, who never lets his dog out of sight. When the dog has raised an animal, the leader announces this and immediately the hunters stand still and wait, bows drawn, for the game to come out. If it is only wounded, the tracking begins. The dog plunges on to the trail, until it stops the game and a hunter brings it down. This hunt is always completed in a few hours; the hunters do not set out until the sun has dissipated the dew, and they return to camp before dusk.

The hunting dog is the Mbuti's only domesticated animal. Nowadays it is obtained from the neighboring farmers. It is the usual kind of bush dog, with a pointed nose, long legs, short, yellowish hair, and has the peculiarity of not barking.

The big hunt, in which the women and children of the camp take part, occurs more rarely. With a great din, the beaters drive the game towards the hunters, who are in ambush ready to shoot arrows at the game chased out by the noise. Sometimes the hunters extend nets which may form a line hundreds of yards long.

According to whether it is in the tropical forest, the wooded savanna or the desert, the optimal number of persons who can effectively hunt together and live on the products of the hunt varies, but in each environment this number is fairly constant. One or two nuclear families, consisting of a hunter, his wife or wives and their children could not subsist alone. An illness, an accident, the failure of a hunter would be enough to place the whole group in danger. On the other hand, too great a number of hunters would too soon use up the hunting territory close to the camp. They would have to hunt far away or move camp very frequently. Thus the conditions of obtaining food establish numerical limits which the hunting band cannot exceed without losing its effectiveness.

Band and Camp

This harmony between the size of the work group and the prerequisites for effective work is a rather general phenomenon, but in other societies the group of technical cooperation usually does not coincide with the unit which develops for other social activities such as sharing of consumer goods, control of individual behavior, even in family relationships, education and discipline of children, ritual ceremonies. The hunting band—a group for technical cooperation—with its dependents, women, children and the aged, forms a social universe, its material expression being the camp. Dwellings are of flimsy materials: they consist of huts in the forest, windbreaks in the savannas, or simply natural shelters such as caves. The camp is never permanent, for even an optimal group cannot remain for long in the same place without exhausting the game and vegetable resources.

The camp constitutes a unit of consumption. Game is shared unequally between the various families of a camp, but every family gets a share. Among certain Bushman groups the sharing obeys very exact rules: one piece is reserved for the hunter's wife, another for the chief, another for the close relatives of the hunter. Among the Naron, studied by Isaac Schapera, the animal is cut up where it is killed and the liver is eaten by the hunters; the sharing-out takes place at the camp: the wife of the hunter who has killed the animal receives the fat, the hindquarters and the entrails; she cooks this part, then gives some to the other women in the camp. The rest of the animal is spread out under the tree in the middle of the camp; the hunter receives the ribs and one of the shoulders, and he cooks them on his personal fire or the men's fire according to very precise rules; he eats them in the company of the other men with whom he usually hunts. The leader of the hunt receives a two-inch strip cut from each limb, which he must eat by himself. The rules for sharing vary in different hunting groups, but the important principle is that all the members of the group benefit from the catch of each member. In the uncertainty of hunting life, this is an important security.

How does a person enter into this group with its tight-knit social relationships? First, by birth. A hunter's sons are trained by their father from their early youth in the techniques and skills of hunting. When they reach adult age and are married they usually continue to hunt with their father. However, free choice also plays a part: a hunter may leave a group and be admitted to another. This is often the result of disputes or particular affinities. Thus it may happen that two brothers belong to different bands.

The social unit of the civilization of the bow surprised political scientists because it seems to exemplify political anarchy, that is, the absence of any government, any political authority. And for classical political philosophy it seems impossible for a society to function without authority. But first, is it quite certain that hunters have no chiefs? It is reported that certain Bushman groups recognize the power to decide certain important matters, such as the choice of a camp site, as belonging to one person, and this function may become hereditary; it is also stated that the most skillful hunter gains ascendancy over his companions—which is quite natural—and they follow him in the hunt. Colin M. Turnbull, who shared the life of several bands of the Mbuti of the Ituri, discovered no chiefs among them, and he reports the statement of an old Pygmy who said that if the neighboring farmers have chiefs the Mbuti do not have them. Even if some forest hunters are not subject to any political authority, the sociological problem remains unsolved: how have these groups been able to make their members conform to the basic social rules—not to kill, steal, etc.—without which a society cannot be maintained? Actually such conformity is obtained by an authority which threatens potential delinquents with precise sanctions, to be applied by force. When there is no coercive authority sanctions of this type, called political sanctions, do not exist.

Cephu, a hunter of the Ituri forest, liked to erect his hut of branches a little apart from the camp and did not participate fully in collective life. One day, when the whole camp had organized a hunt in which the game was to be driven into nets, his un-cooperative behavior went beyond the limits. As usual before a collective undertaking, the hunt fire was lit some distance from the camp, a rite of offering and prayer to the forest, giver of all. Cephu was the only one of the hunters who was not there. He arrived late, when the nets had already been set up and the first antelope had been brought down. When the meat was shared out on the spot he was not offered any part. Later, Cephu complained very loudly that he had not killed any game because the women deliberately drove the game away from his nets. The women answered back, and these altercations created a tense atmosphere and very soon put an end to the hunt.

When the hunters returned to the camp, in small groups, it was learned that Cephu had done something even more reprehensible. He had moved his nets in front of the line of the other nets, which had enabled him to catch animals that were running away. In this way he had killed a few and had hidden them so he could keep them. But what he had hoped to do in secret had been noticed. That was a very serious offence, for it threatened the cooperation of the hunting band which could survive only by a system of reciprocal obligations which guaranteed each member a share in the day's catch. Ekianga and Manyalibo, who had caught Cephu, shouted out very loud what they thought of such conduct, and said that the camp site would have to be abandoned. This was a very serious question and would have to be settled at once.

Everybody gathered together and Cephu was called. When he arrived everybody was busy settling in, and, very deliberately, they pretended not to notice him. He went towards a young man who was sitting on a stool. As Cephu was much older, the seat would have been offered to him immediately in normal circumstances. He did not dare to ask the young hunter for it, and the young man remained seated with conspicuous nonchalance. Cephu went towards another stool, on which Amabosu was sitting. As Amabosu ignored him, he shook him. The answer was that animals sit on the ground. This was too much for Cephu, who began a long tirade in which he recalled that he was one of the oldest hunters in the group and that he could not be treated as an animal. Masisi, a relative of Cephu, intervened, and Amabosu gave up his stool to Cephu. Then Manyalibo got up and expressed all the grievances which Cephu's behavior had caused at the last camp. Finally he came to that day's incident, the stolen meat. This violation of solidarity evoked manifestations of anger from everybody, and Cephu began to weep. He tried feebly to explain that he had lost contact with the others and this was how his net had been found in front of the line. Knowing that nobody believed him, he added that in any case he deserved a better position in the line of nets. After all, was he not an important man, the chief of his own band?

A hunter replied that it was not necessary to prolong the discussion: since he was a chief he was a villager, for the Mbuti never have chiefs; since he had his own band, let him go elsewhere and be its chief. . . . Cephu realized that he was defeated and humiliated. His band of three or four families was too small to form an effective hunting team alone. He apologized, repeating that he really did not know that he had placed his nets in front of the others, and that in any case he would give back all the meat. This put an end to the discussion.

Accompanied by most of the hunters, he returned to his hut, which was a little apart from the others, and told his wife to give away all the meat. All was immediately taken. Even the pot that was on the fire was emptied. He protested, but everybody laughed at him. He cried that he would starve, but they only laughed more. In the evening, when Masisi had finished his meal, he took a pot of meat cooked by his wife and slipped away in the darkness in the direction of the hut of his kinsman Cephu. Later in the night when the hunters were singing the *molimo*, Cephu was among them.

Diffuse Sanctions by Social Pressure

This story, reported by Turnbull, shows very clearly how the group can very effectively put pressure on anybody who violates the rules, without the existence of a coercive authority. The ostracism with which Cephu was threatened is an extremely serious sanction, for an ostracized hunter cannot survive alone for long, but must quickly gain admittance to another band. But what band would be willing to receive a person so asocial that he had got himself expelled from his own group? Thus the threat of ostracism is most often sufficient: the delinquent soon submits. There are other forms of social pressure: scorn and ridicule. They may seem ineffective to a person who lives in a society where people do not all know each other personally and where they do not live all the time in contact with one another. In such large and complex societies it is possible to avoid, more or less, those who conspicuously ignore you or laugh at you. One can at least take refuge at home for some of the time each day. In the communal life of a forest camp, this is impossible: people live very close together, they need each other, and everything is known to everybody. Even at night one has only to raise one's voice a little for the whole camp to know about the most intimate quarrels. In these conditions, to be ostracized or to be constantly a laughing-stock very soon makes life intolerable. That is why group pressure, although diffuse, makes a very effective sanction.

Sanctions are moderate and devoid of brutality because they pre-suppose the unanimous agreement of the group. For if anybody thinks the sanction too severe and does not fully participate in the common attitude of disapproval, the sanction immediately loses its strength and effectiveness. The whole group must fully approve the collective attitude. Thus people tend to range themselves with the more moderate rather than with the more severe.

Reconciliation for Cooperation

Indeed, the group does not wish to separate itself from one of its members unless he seems truly irredeemable. The main aim is to reconcile, to re-create the conditions which allow social cooperation. Any disagreement, in so close and tight-knit a group, soon ceases to be a matter between two individuals. The whole group is involved. It is therefore important to restore social harmony as soon as possible.

Aberi and Masalito were brothers. Aberi, the elder, was aggressive and ugly; his wife Tamasa was disfigured by yaws. He considered himself the head of the lineage, although Masalito was recognized to be more intelligent, a better hunter, a better singer, a better dancer and to have a prettier wife. This situation naturally caused a tense relationship between the two brothers. Thanks to Masalito, who liked peace, the appearance of good relations was maintained between the brothers. One rainy afternoon when nobody was hunting, Masalito went to visit his brother. Aberi was asleep, and Masalito sat down with Tamasa, his sister-in-law, and asked her for something to smoke with. She gave him a baked clay pipe bowl, a little tobacco, and, for a pipe-stem, a long rib freshly cut from the middle of a banana leaf. Tamasa had recently been in a peasant village and had brought back several of these ribs, which make excellent pipe stems. Masalito drew a few puffs, then passed the pipe to Tamasa. But instead of accepting it she roughly knocked it over, spilling on the ground the rest of the tobacco. It was a deliberate insult. Masalito, not wanting to aggravate the situation, gave Tamasa the opportunity to reestablish good relations: he asked her for another pipe stem to take home with him. To refuse the request from her husband's brother would be a serious act of hostility, while if she gave him the banana-rib the previous insult would be wiped out.

"Of course I'll give you one," she said, and she went to fetch from a heap of garbage behind the hut an old pipe stem which was so much used that it had been thrown away there. Masalito, insulted a second time, got angry, and called Tamasa names which are not fitting for a man to apply to the wife of his older brother. Upon which, Aberi awoke, and Masalito, in a rage, insulted him and hit him with the old pipe stem. Then, brandishing it, Masalito returned to his own hut, hurling insults in the direction of his brother and sister-in-law and telling the whole story. The old pipe stem was a proof which won Masalito every-body's sympathy. Aberi, furious in his turn, arrived shortly afterwards, demanding apologies. Masalito, now quite composed, simply threw the old pipestem at his brother's feet. Aberi threatened to hit his brother. Masalito retorted that he had better get his spear and kill him if he dared. This made Aberi even angrier, and he went into a sort of dance, showing how he would kill his brother as soon as he had got his spear. In executing this mime, he leaped in a way which he would have liked to be most impressive, but, not being a good dancer, he missed his step and fell flat on his face. Everybody burst out laughing, and for weeks he was asked if he had lost his spear and reminded to be careful and to watch not to fall.

Masalito meanwhile was not satisfied. The ridicule that Aberi had incurred reflected to some degree on the whole family so that relations between the two brothers only got worse. Masalito took advantage of every opportunity to express his resentment publicly. This never-ending quarrel became a threat to public peace, for Masalito urged his friends and kinsmen to adopt a very hostile attitude towards Aberi. That was when the *molimo* stepped in.

For the uninitiated, that is, women and children, the *molimo* is an animal of the forest which manifests itself on certain nights by uttering strange sounds all around the camp; sometimes he even goes through the camp. Women and children are not allowed to see him and must stay shut up in the huts. One night the *molimo* shook and slightly damaged Masalito's hut. This made him too look foolish, and he understood. A day or two later the two brothers were hunting together.

This episode, which was observed by Turnbull, shows clearly that when disputes occur it is more important to put pressure on the adversaries to settle the matter than to see that each one gets his rights. Although everybody considered that Masalito was in the right at first, social pressure, put into action by the use of the *molimo*, was used against him when it appeared that it was his obstinacy which prevented a reconciliation with his brother, which was necessary if the camp was to continue to cooperate effectively.

In this way social control can be exercised in a small group with no political organization. Underlying apparent chaos is an order ensured by very flexible sanctions, which make large allowances for individual personalities and social relationships. Thus we find among forest hunters, with their harsh way of life, a delicate sense of interpersonal relationships. The following story illustrates how careful they are to avoid losing face or causing somebody else to lose face. After a quarrel with her husband, a woman began methodically to remove the leaf roof of their hut. This was acceptable behavior, for the woman builds the hut and it is considered as her property. Usually the husband intervenes to calm her, but this husband was especially obstinate and he let her pull off all the leaves. All he did was to remark loudly enough for the whole camp to hear that his wife would be very cold that night. There was nothing for her to do but continue: reluctantly and very slowly she began to pull out the sticks that formed the framework of the house. She was in tears, for she loved her husband, and if he did not stop her all she could do would be to pack up her few personal possessions and return to the home of her parents. The husband seemed anxious too; they had both gone too far to make up their quarrel without losing face in the eyes of the camp, where everybody was waiting with curiosity to see how the matter would end. When there were only a few sticks left to be pulled out, the husband's face suddenly lit up and he told his wife not to bother pulling out the sticks as only the leaves were dirty. She looked dumbfounded, then, understanding, asked him to help her carry the leaves to the river. They gravely washed every leaf, brought them back, and the woman happily rebuilt the hut, pretending she had taken off the leaves, not because she was angry, but simply because they were dirty and attracted ants and spiders. Of course nobody believed them, but for several days the women talked about insects in their huts and took off a few leaves to wash them in the river, though this action was very unusual.

This supremacy of social cohesion, which is shown by the stress on persuasion rather than force and by a certain gentleness in personal relationships, gives way to rougher practices when environmental conditions are or become harsher. Thus in the very severe conditions of the Kalahari, when the survival of the band is in danger if it cannot move swiftly to a waterhole, it may happen that an old man is abandoned.

Beyond the Camp

The social horizon of the hunter is not bounded by the group which hunts and camps together. There are relationships between different groups, especially with regard to marriage. The universal rule of exogamy forces one to find a spouse in a group other than one's own. This, of course, is a kinship group, and a hunting band is not composed entirely of descendants of the same ancestor. However, if several of the sons and grandsons of a hunter continue to hunt together, the number of relatives amongst whom the incest prohibition holds will become rather high in a band, and people will have to seek marriage partners elsewhere. Also, there are neighborly relations between bands hunting in adjacent territories, and the reputation of a pretty girl quickly spreads and attracts suitors. When a marriage has been decided on between two camps, the girl goes to live with her husband, who usually continues to hunt with his father. But she returns to her parents for fairly long visits. Thus bonds between groups are created and maintained on the matrimonial level. These bonds are further strengthened among the Mbuti where exchange marriage is practised. This is in effect a double marriage, the ideal form of which is that a brother and sister of group A marry a sister and brother of group B. This means that when a man wants to marry a certain girl, he has to arrange at the same time another marriage bewteen one of his sisters or kinswomen and the brother or a kinsman of the girl he wants to marry. The two marriages thus have a sort of solidarity, and create between the two groups a strong bond which both are interested in maintaining.

On the other hand, neighborly relations between different hunting bands are not always friendly. During periods of drought, when game becomes scarce, each band strongly defends the rights it claims to hunt in the less dry areas where some vegetation still remains. It is also reported of the Bushmen that at certain times of the year ceremonial activities may bring several bands together, but there is no political authority extending over more than one band. It is because they have the same way of life that the hunters of a region feel themselves as different from the farmers or herdsmen, and also because they are Negritos or Khoisans, that is, physically different from the "tall black men."

The Forest as Providence

Hunting and gathering do not change the natural environment in any way. The world in which the band lives supplies the necessities of life. Even if it is hard and difficult to obtain food, that food comes as a gift. This is how the world is experienced by hunters. For the Mbuti, this experience is expressed in a very conscious attitude of dependence and love towards the forest, which is for them protective rather than hostile. This attitude is clearly shown by the *molimo* ritual. This mysterious animal of the forest screams and sings at night around and in the camp when anybody dies or, on the other hand, when something fortunate happens. It is, as all initiates, that is, all adult men, know, a wooden cylinder with which some of the young hunters run through the camp, and which amplifies the voice of one of them. An old Mbuti hunter explained the meaning of the ritual in these terms to Turnbull: "Normally, all goes well in our world. But at night, when we are asleep, sometimes things go wrong because we are not awake to prevent them from going wrong. An army of ants invades the camp, leopards may come and carry off a hunting dog or even a child. If we were awake, these things would not happen. So when something important goes wrong, such as an illness, an unsuccessful hunt or a death, this must be because the forest is asleep and is not taking care of her children. So what do we do? We wake her up. We wake her up by singing, because we want her awakening to be pleasant. Then everything goes well again. And when our world goes well, we sing to the forest then, too, because we want her to share our happiness."

The Mbuti have different names for their god. If they conceive this divinity as distinct from the forest, they see it in the form of the forest. She is good, no particular favor is asked of her, simply to watch over her children. And when some disaster happens, confidence is not shaken. As the *molimo* song goes: "All is dark around us, but if the darkness is the darkness of the forest, then the darkness must be good."

The civilization of the bow is a complete way of life, organized around a certain way of obtaining subsistence. Despite its material poverty, it is a good adaptive solution for a group of men in their environment, since it has enabled humanity to survive for thousands of years, and since it has provided a harmonious and satisfying frame of reference for individuals, as far as we can tell judging from the few contemporary hunting societies. New techniques—agriculture, herding, manufacture—will enable men to extract from the natural environment more than can be obtained by hunting and gathering, and the civilization of the bow will retreat and become marginal. Nowadays, Pygmies and Bushmen carry on numerous trade relationships with neighboring groups of Black peasants. Though these consist mainly of exchange of agricultural produce and iron objects for wild meat, in some cases the relationship is so close that it may be called symbiosis. In the Ituri forest, the Blacks organize and direct the initiation of both Black and Pygmy boys at the same times, according to their ritual. To live from nature without changing it is a doomed technique. In Africa it has lasted until now only in the area where the natural environment presents great obstacles to agricultural utilization. This situation cannot persist for long in the Africa of the second half of the twentieth century.

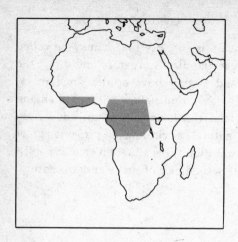

THE CIVILIZATION
OF THE CLEARINGS

Sculpture of the Great Forest

An observer looking down from a low-flying plane on to the great equatorial forest with its huge trees, its dense, tangled vegetation, its giant roots that rise many feet above the ground, its foliage always green and luxuriant, its frightening intensity of vegetable growth, may glimpse few gaps, rare and far apart. These are the clearings cut by forest cultivators.

These forest farmers are amazing sculptors. More than any other African peoples they have created those statues, for a long time called fetishes, representing men and women in an abstract but lifelike style, with proportions strange to us but integrated into a coherent whole, motionless, but always ready to move. If we superimpose on a vegetation map of Africa a map indicating the places where traditional sculpture developed, the crescent of the great forest and that of sculpture coincide to a very high degree; the latter, however, extends a little further than the former.

The southern limit of the canopy forest is about the fourth parallel south of the equator; it extends eastward to the Great Lakes rift and the high plateaus of Tanzania, Burundi, Rwanda and Uganda; northward it gives way to savanna about the fourth parallel also, but to the north-west it continues beyond the Niger delta, and, after a gap around the Bight of Benin, extends westward along the coastal forests in the south of Ghana, the Ivory Coast, Liberia and part of Sierra Leone. The most typical forest zone is in the "central basin," the lowlands of the Congo and its tributaries, especially the Ubangi. The Atlantic forest provides a very similar environment, but it differs from the equatorial region because of two influences: the proximity of the ocean and distance from the equator. Between the fourth and eighth parallels, the climate is not yet tropical—characterized by a dry season and a rainy season—but the difference between maximum and minimum rainfall widens to the point when, though one cannot yet speak of a dry season, one can yet speak of a rainy season. On her map of the distribution of sculpture, Denise Paulme extends the "fertile crescent" of Black art beyond the forest zone; but the forest still runs down the middle of it.

The human figures carved by the farmers of the clearings are quite varied. In the Congo (Kinshasa) alone, Frans M. Olbrechts distinguishes five great stylistic regions and about twenty styles and sub-styles. On the basis of tribal characteristics, Ladislas Segy estimates that African sculptures can be arranged in a classification of about two hundred styles. However, these statues have common features and it is very rarely that one cannot guess their African origin at first sight. Thus they are usually carved in cylindrical form. The reason for this is the sculptor's technique: he starts with a single block, a tree trunk

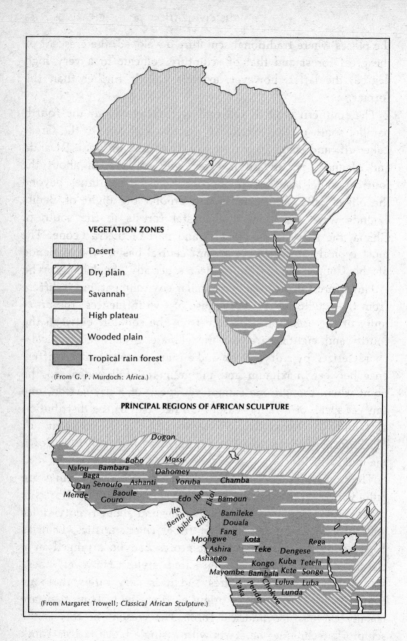

VEGETATION ZONES

- Desert
- Dry plain
- Savannah
- High plateau
- Wooded plain
- Tropical rain forest

(From G. P. Murdoch: *Africa*.)

PRINCIPAL REGIONS OF AFRICAN SCULPTURE

Dogon

Bobo   Mossi
Nalou Bambara   Dahomey
Baga
Dan Senoufo Ashanti Yoruba   Chamba
Mende   Baoule
Gouro   Edo Ibo   Bamoun
Ife   Ekoi
Benin   Bamileke
Ibibio Efik   Douala
Mpongwe   Fang
Ashira   Kota Teke Dengese   Rega
Ashango   Kongo Kuba Tetela
Mayombe Bambala   Kete Songe
Yaka Pende Chokwe Lulua Luba
Lunda

(From Margaret Trowell; *Classical African Sculpture*.)

or branch which he cuts down with an axe, an adze or a knife; he rarely adds a piece to the original block. Within the narrow limits set by this technique the artist must resolve the problems of three-dimensional design.

The body is straight, the spine perfectly vertical and the head is an extension of the trunk, on exactly the same axis. The arms, which are also cylindrical, are rarely separate from the body. The body is symmetrical right and left. These characteristics suggest the column; they give to African statues, even small ones, a monumentality, a strength, a power, which make a great impression on the viewer.

The legs are too short in relation to the body; the thigh and the lower leg make a very sharp angle at the knee. This is not a position of rest; on the contrary, it suggests the tension immediately preceding an imminent movement. These characteristics express a restrained dynamism.

The faces do not have individual features; and one can rarely find in them the physical characteristics of a race. From a figure with a long, thin nose, a small mouth with the lips barely indicated, we can infer nothing about the proportions of the face typical of the tribe in which the statue was carved. The expression of the face is never smiling, it is most often very stern. The sculpture is not anecdotal, it does not describe a definite action, it does not tell a story. These features put individuals on the level of abstraction: they are primarily the three-dimensional expression of the idea of man or woman. The absence of particular features however does not detract from the vivacity of this art; it is just the opposite of cold or unemotional: these sculptured "ideas" exist intensely. Sexual characteristics are carved very clearly. The round and angular shapes which contrast with and balance one another in very many statues suggest almost unconsciously the essence of womanhood or manhood. African sculpture is a strongly and deeply sexual art. This does not make it less austere: sex is here associated with fertility rather than pleasure. Pregnant women and women in labor are sometimes represented. African sculpture is expressionist. It does not seek to represent the visual impression but to express what the artist conceives intellectually and feels emotionally. If it can be included among the few great artistic traditions of the world, it is certainly not because of its content but because of its form. The forest sculptors—not all of them, they have also produced many mediocre works—have succeeded in creating rhythmic and balanced shapes in which masses and planes form perfectly integrated wholes. It is therefore not in the least surprising that the aesthetic value of African art was discovered by Western artists before anthropologists. At the beginning of the twentieth century the sculptors and painters of the Paris school found in "Negro art" the confirmation that a great art could develop in a direction other than that of academic realism. These men, women and, sometimes, couples are statues of ancestors. This fact underlines the primary importance which the men of the clearings attribute to kinship. Through kinship an individual finds his place in society; kinship determines his various forms of behavior towards each category of his blood relations and relatives by marriage; kinship puts him into a group of solidarity and protection. The forest farmer is above all the descendant of an ancestor.

This relationship must be determined socially, not just biologically. If we took into consideration only biological descent, each individual would be situated at the apex of an inverted triangle the base of which would double every generation: two parents, four grandparents, eight great-grandparents, and so on. This means that even in a quite large group the stage would soon come in which all individuals had the same ancestors; this would not enable any kinship distinctions to be established. Therefore each society gives recognition to only one line of descent and neglects the others. Most of the forest peoples are patrilineal, that is, in determining the descent of an individual they take account only of the male line: his father, his father's father, etc. In such a group two persons will consider themselves as relatives, if, when each of them traces back his patrilineal ancestry, they arrive at a common ancestor. If one meets a person one does not know, one places him by his line of descent. Hence the excellent knowledge of long genealogies, which contrasts with the ignorance displayed by the average European about his ancestors more than a few generations back. For the European uses other frames of reference to estabish the social position of an individual: social class, profession, income, national origin, place of residence, etc.

It is important for a member of a small society to know his consanguineal relationships (that is, blood relationships by descent and collaterality) and his affinal relationships (that is, relationships based on alliances and marriages), for they determine his various roles as son, husband, father, paternal nephew, cross cousin, parallel cousin, uncle, son-in-law, etc. Each of these roles is defined by obligations and rights which establish very precisely how he must conduct himself towards his various kinsfolk, and what he may expect from them.

Kinship Roles

For the Kissi, forest farmers who live at the meeting-point of the boundaries of Guinea, Sierra Leone and Liberia—an area at the north-west edge of the Atlantic forest zone—the role of father is described thus by Denise Paulme: "The father is obligated to feed his children, and to clothe them according to his means; he must consult the diviner if the child falls ill and carry out the sacrifices which the diviner deems necessary for the cure. A man has nothing much to worry about as long as his father is still alive, for his father takes care of everything: farm work, offerings to the ancestors . . . all the responsibilities fall on him, whether they are judicial, economic or ritual. For the son, the death of the father marks the end of an easy life, but also of a state of dependence which may arouse in a man a feeling of suppressed irritation. On the other hand, as a father loses his strength, his son becomes his only support. In the relationship between an old man and his adult son, the feeling of mutual dependence is often accompanied by a latent hostility. The ambiguity of this relationship explains, especially, the importance of a father's funeral, the supreme expression of filial piety and also the first signal of the independence of the son, free at last and responsible for his actions. The first act of the fully adult man is an act of homage to his ancestors."

The mother, continues Denise Paulme, even when infancy is past, remains the source of all material comfort, the symbol of absolute security, as well as the housekeeper who will satisfy her child's hunger. Though her influence over her sons lessens rapidly as they grow up, her influence over her daughters lasts much longer. Their suitors, frivolous or serious, seek to get into her good graces.

Towards paternal uncles, the required attitude is that of respect: but this respect may cover feelings which may range from close affection to near indifference. Between grandparents and grandchildren, the relationship is one of intimacy and confidence, modified by the respect due to old people. Joking is frequent between old men and children, and the alternation of generations creates a sort of silent pact in which grandfather and grandson stand together against the father. The hostility inevitable between an aging father and his son plays no part here. The identification between grandfather and grandson is stressed by the fact that very often the first son of each son receives the name of his paternal grandfather. Thus the old man who has several sons may hope to see his name multiplied in the second generation, and, with his name, his chances of survival. "Between full brother and sister, great intimacy in early childhood gives way at the age of twelve or thirteen to extreme reserve: it is strictly forbidden for a brother to lie down on the mat on which his sister has slept, and vice versa. To get angry with one's sister, to insult or hit her, is an unheard of act, which even a gift of several cola nuts could not expiate. Whatever his sister might demand: skirts, necklaces, etc., the guilty brother may refuse nothing. A brother who catches his sister with a lover says nothing to her: deeply humiliated, he can hardly bring himself to warn their parents."

At the other end of the forest zone, among the Amba who live less than one degree north of the equator at the border of Congo (Kinshasa) and Uganda, Edward H. Winter noted other kinship roles. Between a man and his mother's brother, and reciprocally, between a man and his sister's son, there is a joking relationship. The maternal uncle may laugh at the young man, take liberties with him and even insult him. And the nephew cannot reply in kind but, to compensate, may appropriate any of his uncle's property. He does not have to ask for it; he simply grabs it: for example, if his mother's brother is smoking a new pipe, he can snatch it from him. There is one restriction: if he seizes a live animal, usually a chicken, he must kill it and eat it before he leaves his uncle's home. In this way a man may laugh at his nephew without losing his property, and, on the other hand, one cannot seize anything of one's uncles without allowing oneself to be insulted. Winter also points out that actually people behave reasonably, and usually things are not pushed too far.

One of the Mongo peoples, the Hamba, lives in the great equatorial forest near the River Lomela, a tributary of the Congo. There the nephew has a relationship with his mother's brother similar to that we have described. Luc de Heusch points out other kinship roles. Thus a son-in-law must treat his mother-in-law with great reserve. When he meets her, good manners require that he greet her by modestly turning his head and moving away from her. On the other hand, there are several female affinal relatives whom a man jokingly calls his "wives": the wife of his elder brother, the wife of his maternal uncle. He may joke with them and treat them with great familiarity, but sexual relations with them are prohibited.

The main system of social reference is based on kinship, but it is extended to include persons, living and dead, who are not kinsmen in the strict sense of the term. One kind of extension, which might be called horizontal, operates by assimilating into a certain role—that of father, brother, wife, for example—individuals who occupy similar places by virtue of their generation, age or descent from a common ancestor. Thus a person regards as "his fathers" not only his "real" father, but his father's brothers and patrilateral cousins. Of course, an individual must behave differently towards his father, his father's brothers and his father's more or less distant cousins, but towards each member of this class of persons he will show an attitude of respect, and he will address each of them as "father." This practice was once incorrectly interpreted by some nineteenth-century anthropologists as a confirmation of their fantasy-hypothesis of primitive promiscuity, a situation in which all the men of a group could have sexual relationships with all the women of the group, nobody could identify his father, and consequently everybody addressed as father any man of the previous generation!

By the same principle of classificatory extension, a man's patrilateral parallel cousins (the daughters of his father's brothers) are classed with his sisters and he is obliged to treat them with great reserve, while his patrilateral cross cousins (the daughters of his father's sisters) are not classed with them, for they do not belong to the same lineage as he. In everyday life, classificatory kinship facilitates relationships between different households. Denise Paulme notes that among the Kissi, "in a well-run settlement, occupied by one lineage, the children move freely from one woman's home to another's, since they are the sons and daughters, real or classificatory, of all the women. The men are at home everywhere: their neighbors are their fathers, brothers or sons, the women are their mothers, sisters, wives, daughters or daughters-in-law. Among themselves the women are a little more reserved: their relationships are indirect, depending on the marriage bond, unless two of them come from the same lineage and are thus 'sisters' or 'mother and daughter' according to their relative ages."

Another extension, this one vertical, traces back genealogies beyond the known links, to a mythical ancestor. This makes it possible to declare kinship, sometimes fictitious, between the many living members of a clan or even of a tribe. Thus all the Mongo—who live in the vast forest region between the Congo to the north and the west, the Kasai to the south, and the Lualaba to the east and comprise almost one and a half million individuals—say they are all descended from a single ancestor, Mongo. Their society is composed of a collection of chains of grandfathers, fathers and sons, whose common origin is, they say, the ancestor Mongo. As de Heusch observes, "history is a long list of names and genealogies, confused by distance and seniority rivalries, a succession of rivers crossed, slow journeyings between rivers an endless series of reshufflings." But all the Mongo are brothers because they are sons of Mongo.

Lineages

While each kinship role is expressed by a specific pattern of behavior towards kinsmen, the group consisting of descendants of one ancestor constitutes a closed, organically tight solitary society, which presents a united front to other groups of the same order. These groups—lineages—bring together all those who can trace through real, not fictive, links, the lines of descent that lead back to the same ancestor, who is recognized as the origin of the group. A lineage can function effectively only if the number of its members does not become too large. As the members multiply with each generation, the ancestor who forms the point of reference must be changed fairly often, so that the depth of the lineage may remain more or less the same. This depth is between four and six generations for the Mongo. When the group becomes too large, fission occurs, always based on the principle of descent; instead of considering themselves as sons of Ngeri, their ancestors of the seventh generation, the members of the new group thenceforth call themselves sons of Mbera, their great-great-grandfather, who was a famous great-grandson of Ngeri. They still do not fail to recognize their descent relationship to Ngeri, but the group which will work together; and, in a certain way, live together, will be the lineage of Mbera.

What are the communal activities of the lineage? In the economic sphere, the lineage is rarely a production unit; that consists of the family, which, for the forest farmers, consists of a man, his wife or wives, and their unmarried children. Winter states that among the Amba the couple can carry out nearly all essential economic activities, except house construction. But though routine farming activities can be performed within the framework of the family, this is not so for those which require the cooperation of several men. And such activities are important and numerous, comprising all operations which transform an area of dense forest into a cultivable clearing and enable a village to be established there. A family's right to use a parcel of land is conferred by the lineage: the senior man of the lineage, representing the ancestors, allots to each man the piece of land which he will cultivate for the support of his family.

All the members of a lineage are brothers and comrades. This solidarity is strikingly shown when a wrong has been committed against one of its members by a person outside the group, but its main importance arises from the security it provides with regard to the necessities of daily life. The murder of a son of their ancestor is felt by the whole lineage, and it may be avenged upon any member of the murderer's lineage. But though such mobilizations of the lineage are exceptions because the acts which give rise to them are rare, help from lineage brothers occurs much more often in the case of a bad harvest or other difficulties of economic life. This is very important, when hardly more than is required for current consumption is produced. The knowledge that you will not suffer hunger as long as the whole group does not go hungry, that your wives and children will not be forsaken, even if you are away for a long time or disappear, precludes some sources of anxiety common in more individualistic societies.

The ancestor cult merely reflects on the ritual level the knowledge that each man has of being what he is solely because he is a member of a descent group: everything comes to him down this chain of ancestors represented by the head of the lineage, who is usually its senior man. A simple altar amidst the houses of the living, frequent modest offerings, family prayers, keep the presence of the fathers felt among their children. Life in the world beyond is meager and austere, thus the ancestors are often harsh in temperament, and their bad moods must be appeased; sometimes they escape from this twilight world by reincarnating themselves in one of their descendants. Thus among the Kissi, the shadow, one of the three elements that constitute a living being—the two others are the body and the heart—leaves the body temporarily during sleep and abandons it forever at death; this shadow enters into another body at the moment of birth. The ancestor who has thus returned to his descendants is recognized by the child's features at birth, or by the mother's dreams during her pregnancy. Though the ancestor's shadow has found a new bodily support, the new individual still has a personality different from that of his ancestor, and is not confused with the ancestor. These beliefs and rituals translate the existence of the solidarity of the lineage into reality as lived by its members.

The Marriage Cycle

An individual's social universe is not limited to his lineage. The lineage, a group of descendants in the male line from one father (we are still dealing with the patrilineal system, which is the most common among the forest peoples) must, in order to perpetuate itself, seek wives from other lineages. For men cannot marry the girls of their own lineage, since they are their sisters. So women must come from other lineages, which also need wives from the outside. Thus lineages can persist only by the circulation of women. Wives are so important for the survival of kinship groups that they cannot leave marriage to the hazard of individual inclinations; these matters, as with the European dynasties before the French Revolution, concern the whole group.

The simplest form of marriage regulation is the exchange of women, as among bands of forest hunters. Thus among the Hamba, when a man marries a woman he must give his sister or his daughter in marriage to the father or brother of his bride. As it is often difficult to fulfill the conditions of such an exchange, father, brother, sister and daughter may be replaced by any member of the lineage of the appropriate age and sex. Thus each lineage bestows on another this essential benefit of fertility, while losing nothing itself, for it receives an equivalent benefit. But in other respects marriage by exchange presents serious difficulties: parallel marriage partners cannot always be found; problems which may cause the dissolution of the marriage of one of the couples may very well have repercussions on the parallel couple.

Another marriage system which avoids these drawbacks also exists among the Hamba: this is marriage by compensation, which is the most common form among the forest farmers. The bridegroom gives certain goods to the person who represents the lineage of his bride. Among the Hamba, this is a certain number of goats or sheep, between six and sixteen; among the Mongo, metal goods of iron, copper or brass; among the Kissi, skeins of spun cotton. These goods were sometimes considered as the purchase price of a woman. In the traditional culture of the forest clearings, the meaning of these marriage gifts is clear: the lineage requesting a woman, instead of giving in exchange another woman, offers goods which enable the lineage which bestows the woman to obtain another woman in its turn. Thus the problem of simultaneous parallel marriages is avoided, and the circulation of marriage partners is much broader, since it is no longer limited to two lineages only. This interpretation is confirmed by the fact that among certain groups the goods obtained from the marriage of a daughter may be used only to obtain a wife for one of the men of the lineage.

Village Government

Lineages cooperate with each other in other ways besides matrimonial alliances. They must also come to an understanding about the administration and government of the villages. Often, in fact, members of several lineages live in the same village. Traveling through Mongo country, notes G. Hulstaert, one notices that the dwellings are grouped into villages which consist either of a simple row of houses, or of two rows, one each side of the path. The patriarchs of the various lineages are equal, but when the lineages are related by kinship—which is common, because of the process of fission we have described—the senior man of the senior lineage enjoys an incontestable precedence of respect. When the origins of the lineages in a village are more heterogeneous, the situation is still not very different from that when the lineages are related, for one lineage has always arrived first, then others have been authorized to settle there and have thus recognized the supremacy of the first.

Denise Paulme tells us that Kissi villages often have less than fifty inhabitants, rarely more than two hundred, divided between two or three lineages. Thus a certain number of the inhabitants are descendants of the founder of the village. In a settlement of some size, the lineages tend to group together in one place, sometimes forming distinct quarters of the village, sometimes separate altogether.

The forest farmers usually live in villages which are so far apart that frequent communication between them is not easy. These communities are small: H. Van Geluwe notes that among the Bira—who live in the Epulu forest on either side of the first parallel north in the east of Congo (Kinshasa)—the villages comprise on the average twenty households. They must often include a mixture of lineages, and their government is based on the kinship principle: the head of the senior or the longest established lineage presides at the meetings of the other lineage heads. Thus matters affecting the village are arranged by negotiation, while each lineage head decides autonomously in matters internal to his lineage. Thus the government of villages and their hinterlands does not depend on the territorial principle (by which the chief has authority over all those who live in his territory), but essentially on the kinship principle (by which the patriarch has authority over all those who are descended from a certain ancestor). This is one of the reasons why the forest farmers, even when they speak the same language, have the same beliefs, recognize a common mythical ancestor, have hardly ever formed political units larger than the village. It is difficult for the kinship principle to be the basis of organization of a centralized state. But there are other, strongly determining reasons for the absence of state organization; these arise from the way the forest habitat is utilized.

Cultivators

The men of the clearings are cultivators. They have a very different attitude towards nature from that of the hunters and gatherers: they are not content to take what the forest offers them, but they change it, they sow in order to reap. For them the forest is not the all-giving mother, she is the enemy force against which they struggle to wrest and keep the earth in the clearings. In the various rituals, the opposition between the world of the forest and nature and the world of the village and culture is very clearly expressed. Yet forest farming gives a very modest yield: the soil is poor, although the luxurious natural vegetation might suggest the opposite, conditions of life are hard and unhealthy—tools seem so few and simple to perform the enormous task of clearing the equatorial forest.

In his study of the equatorial habitat, Pierre Gourou points out some of the chemical and physical reasons for the poverty of the soil in this zone. It is greatly lacking in bases and assimilable phosphorus. Its acidity is not favorable for efficient utilization of humus. Also, the topsoil is thin, so that the clearing of a forest area produces sandy layers on which even the forest vegetation can hardly grow again after the soil has been used by man. The copious rain only increases this poverty: it leaches the soil, carrying away nitrates and bases; termites work the soil, preparing the way for innumerable microorganisms which decompose organic matter. To all these disadvantages must be added the threat of erosion by the streaming rain water, and the formation of laterite, the leprosy of soil.

The rain forest is a very unhealthy habitat. One has only to recall the names of a few diseases which are endemic under such conditions: malaria, trypanosomiasis, filariasis, ankylostomiasis, and a whole variety of intestinal diseases. These diseases prevent a population from increasing, and they greatly diminish peoples' capacity for work. They also affect animals, and this is probably the main reason for the absence of stock-raising among the forest farmers. Only small animals are raised: a few hens, one or two goats, sometimes a pig are usually all a family possesses. These animals never form a normal part of the diet: they are sacrificed rather than slaughtered, and eaten on special occasions, such as weddings and funerals.

The axe and the hoe are the basic tools of the forest farmer. In Black Africa they are always made of iron. It is generally agreed that iron-working was introduced into sub-Saharan Africa at the height of the kingdom of Meroe, in the three last centuries B.C. Forest clearing and agriculture are not necessarily bound up with knowledge of iron: in South America, New Guinea and Australia, important territories were cleared solely with polished stone tools. But stone provides such imperfect tools that we must agree with Alfred Métraux in saying that for forest cultivators the introduction of iron constituted a revolution, the revolution of the axe. This importance of iron is shown in the exceptional position given to blacksmiths in the societies of the forest clearings: master of fire, he is not only a specialized artisan, the only one in the village, he also possesses magical powers for which he is feared and respected.

Agricultural Cycle and Isolation

Clearing takes place in the Atlantic forest during the dry season, and in the equatorial forest during the period when precipitation is lowest. The patriarch of the lineages chooses the sites where the cutting will begin. According to an F.A.O. (Food and Agriculture Organization) expert who studied this process in the Congo basin in the Kisangani region, the spots selected are those where the soil is good for farming and yet not covered with excessively hard trees or too thick vegetation. The work is very arduous and is performed cooperatively by all the men of a lineage or even of a village. They begin by cutting down the underbrush: vines, bushes and grass. Some time later they attack the trees. Hard woods are left. If they produce too much shade they are finally burned standing. To make it easier to cut down large trees, especially those with large buttresses or above-ground roots at the foot, the men build scaffolding and platforms which enable them to chop the trunks five or six yards above ground level, where the diameter is smaller. Since the stumps are not pulled out, when the clearing is completed the ground is covered with an impenetrable mass of cut grasses, branches, vines and huge trunks of great felled trees. Everything is left like this for four to six weeks, to allow the vegetation to dry out. Then it is burned. The forest is so resistant that the enormous fires lit in the clearings hardly affect the untouched edges of the forest.

The women clean up the burned land a little, and proceed to sowing and planting. Various food plants are cultivated, especially root crops (manioc, yams, sweet potatoes). These are found wild in all the forests of the warm regions of the earth, and the forest cultivators possess cultivated varieties of them. Banana trees and palm trees are planted and cereals (rice, eleusine, maize, sorghum, millet) are sown. Cereals and squashes are usually supplementary crops, the main foods being almost always based on roots and bananas. These various species are mixed but are not all planted at the same time. Thus among the Rega in the

Kivu Province of Congo (Kinshasa) rice is first broadcast. When it begins to grow, manioc cuttings are planted at intervals, and, a few weeks later, banana roots.

Once planting is completed, the crop does not usually receive any further attention until harvest. The women do the harvesting, which is usually spread out over a rather long period. The grains are harvested when they are ripe, an ear at a time. Manioc and bananas are left in the fields, where they form a reserve which is drawn upon as needed.

Thus the agricultural cycle is completed, but it can be repeated in the same place only a very few times, not more than two or three, in many areas. This is because the poor soil is quickly exhausted and must lie fallow for a period which may be as long as twenty years. Thus almost every year new parts of the forest must be cleared.

This agricultural nomadism is the material basis of the civilization of the clearings. It sets rather narrow limits on the possible forms of social life. Like all farmers, these forest dwellers tend to be sedentary, but when all the fields around the village are in fallow, it is preferable to move the village rather than be obliged to walk long distances every day. Thus the advantages of stable settlement are not available to forest cultivators.

For the same reason they cannot live in very large groups. The area of land required by this type of agriculture is so large that, for example, the hinterland of a village of a thousand inhabitants would be too extensive to be conveniently utilized. Colonial administrations have often been unwilling or unable to understand this requirement; they have often declared to be unoccupied lands which were temporarily out of use but which would have to be cleared at some later time so that a village could survive. The dense, hostile forest isolates the villages, which are of necessity far apart, since each one moves within a broad zone of past, present and potential land utilization. This isolation has very serious consequences. Protecting the villages from conquest by war, it safeguards the independence of these small, weak communities. Conquerors had to stop at the edges of the forest, which provided a refuge for many a group fleeing from enemies. On the other hand, isolation made it very difficult to constitute political units comprising several villages with the same culture. The forest has a disintegrating effect. Finally—and this is the most harmful effect of isolation in the forest—inventions, new techniques, and ideas from outside can be communicated only imperfectly and with great difficulty. Cultures are enriched much more by such communications than by internal development due to inventions. This is true even of the great cultural traditions such as that of western Europe, which assimilated much more than it created. When a human group, especially a small one, keeps apart from the great mainstreams of the world, its culture remains very static.

This isolation is especially striking in the case of the peoples of the forest clearings, but it also existed in other vast areas of Black Africa. This situation accounts for the relative poverty of certain aspects of African civilizations, especially in the domain of production techniques. It is not because of any intellectual inferiority of Africans that these aspects of their culture have remained rudimentary, but simply because their isolation did not allow them to participate in the intense cultural exchanges centered on the Mediterranean basin. When other human groups lived in similar state of isolation, the effect of this situation on their cultures was the same.

In spite of very harsh ecological conditions, despite the self-centeredness of kinship groups and their solitude in the dense, hostile forest, the cultivators of the clearing managed to subsist and, as we have seen, created a plastic art whose aesthetic quality won a place among the great artistic traditions of the world. This indeed is an astounding and wonderful accomplishment.

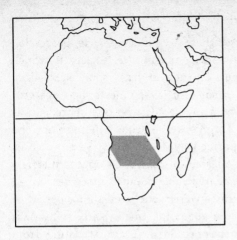

THE CIVILIZATION
OF THE GRANARIES

An Art Style of Opulence and Prestige

The Kuba craftsmen of the savanna make cups in the form of heads, cosmetic boxes, head-rests, pipes, stools, and fabrics of embroidered raffia. In these everyday objects we may discern certain characteristics of forest sculpture: when the material is wood it is worked in the block; human figures are treated in an abstract, expressionist manner; the faces are impersonal and unsmiling. Differences from the sculpture of the clearings are also evident. Here the objects are for secular use, to make ordinary activities pleasanter and more comfortable. Geometric or anthropomorphic decoration is abundant, even overabundant, and very carefully executed: these are luxury objects, possession of which ensures a certain social prestige. A society in which such things are made must include at least some specialized craftsmen, for the finish of some of these objects indicates professional workmanship, and some people who own more than is necessary for subsistence, for in order to acquire these things one must pay the craftsmen in some way.

About 1950, R. Verly collected in some old Kongo cemeteries in northern Angola a very considerable number of statues carved in soft stone. These sculptures were made over a long period of time. In the study he wrote about his finds, Verly notes that some of these statues, mentioned in a document dating from 1514, were brought about 1695 to Rome (where they still are) by an Italian missionary, and that the last stone carvers died about 1910. Although these statues are quite small—their height varies from about twelve to twenty inches—they have an impressively monumental character. Unlike most African sculpture, they are not symmetrical: the back is not always vertical, and often the head is at an angle in relation to the back. These crude statues, with the surface carved in very high relief, seem alive with a deep, calm, thoughtful inner vitality. The head-dresses of most of these personages indicate by stylized symbols —such as leopards' claws—that they occupy a position of authority among the Kongo. Such stone statues are a sign of a society which has crossed the threshold of simple subsistence and is firmly rooted in its territory.

Among the Kongo, the Luba, the Songe and other peoples of the savannas to the south of the great equatorial forest, we admire richly and delicately carved staffs, finely worked adzes, broad-bladed axes attached to the handle by delicately wrought linked mouldings. The ornamentation of these objects has developed to the point where they have become unusable for their ordinary purpose, as walking-sticks, carving tools or cutting tools. They are symbolic objects, intended to represent Power in the most impressive possible manner. These scepters and ceremonial axes can exist only in a society in which the chief has great power, for they show in striking fashion that their owner is much superior to the other men of his people.

Among the Luba art objects that may be seen in European museums, a collection of stools supported by caryatids and Atlantus figures is of considerable interest. Aesthetically they are masterpieces. Also, they may be attributed to the same sculptor, which is rare in African art. The homogeneity of this series, which is called Buli, and its difference from other works in the Luba tradition, lead specialists such as Frans M. Olbrechts to conclude that "this is not a regional sub-style, but certainly the work of one artist, or at least of artists of the same school or workshop." Thus in Luba society the anonymous craftsman has become an artist, and the economic foundation of the society has been adequate to develop workshops devoted to the creation of art and luxury objects.

The Kuba royal statues are famous. They are wooden figures in the round from one to two feet high, representing kings of the Kuba, sitting cross-legged. On the head, which is disproportionately large, is the headdress reserved for royal rank. Though different styles may be distinguished in these statues, especially the archaic features of the sixteenth- and seventeenth-century sculptures, the faces are impersonal. Yet each king may be identified by a symbol in high relief on the pedestal, recalling one of the most characteristic events of his reign. Thus Olbrechts states that if the king was "a famous artist in wrought iron, such as Bope Pelenge (who reigned about 1800) we find an anvil in front of his throne; if the most outstanding act of a king was the repealing of the law forbidding marriage between nobles and slaves, as was the case for Mikope Mbula (who reigned from 1810 to 1840) we find the king represented with a young slave woman in front of his throne; if a king's great merit was to cure his people of a passion for games of chance, by introducing a much more harmless game, lela, as was the case for Shamba Bolongongo (who reigned about 1600-1620), the symbol repre-

sented in front of his throne is one of the little *lela* counters."
This dynastic statuary gives us an insight into history: individual
names and events appear. Even among people without writing,
power, when it achieves the magnitude of royalty, ceases to be
anonymous. Oral traditions and sculptural representations pre-
serve the memory of past greatnesses, which magnify and legitimize present power.

The economic and political facts which are revealed in the
various art forms we have mentioned are very different from
those we met with in the civilizations of the bow and of the
clearings. The habitat of what we call the civilization of the
granaries—we shall see later the reason for this term—extends
over great regions south of the fourth parallel south, where the
great rain forest gradually disappears to give place to the dry forest, the wooded savanna and the grassy savanna; in the eastern
part of the continent, it adjoins the region of the high plateaus between the Indian Ocean and the Great Lakes depression, and
goes almost as far as the ocean near the mouth of the Zambezi;
to the southwest, this savanna zone disappears into the desert
regions of the Kalahari and the Namib. This vast region is characterized less by the uniformity of its vegetation than by the
overwhelming influence of the rains, which impose a pattern of
seasons on the life of nature and of men. Its inhabitants, like
the men of the clearings, are also cultivators and not blessed with
fertile soils. So they employ similar methods: practise long
fallowing, rotation of crops, disturb only the surface of the soil.
They use the same basic tool, the hoe. The plow, unknown to
Black farmers, is unsuitable for most African soils; its blade
cuts too deep, turns up sterile layers of earth and causes more
erosion. However, argriculture in the savanna is more productive than in the clearings, and gives much more importance to
grain crops.

This greater productivity is the result of several factors. Since
clearing the land is not so difficult as in dense forest, the same
number of men can open up much larger areas of cultivable land.

Fertilization allows the use of the same plot for a greater number of years. This fertilization is not effected with manure, because in general there are no large domestic animals, but by burning the land every year—an agricultural technique typical of Africa. It consists of setting fire, about the end of the dry season, to all the dead and wild vegetation which remains on the fields after the harvest, so as to enrich the land with the ashes before sowing. The *chitimene* procedure used by the Bemba of Zambia, represents an extreme form of the burning technique. On the site for a field, they make a two foot deep layer of branches collected from the surrounding land, so that vegetation is cut down from an area six or eight times larger than that of the field. But the damage is limited because the Bemba do not cut down the whole trees; they use only the large branches, so that the trees can grow again. Gourou ends his description by adding that "climbing the trees to cut down the high branches is a sport requiring great courage; the men do it with great daring and rivalry, and accidents are frequent."

Surplus, Granaries and Chiefs

The yield of savanna agriculture must not be overestimated. Every year the period before the harvest is difficult, and at this time there may be several weeks of scarcity. And even during the rest of the year, the diet leaves much to be desired. Diseases of undernourishment, such as kwashiorkor, are common among African peasants, as much the result of an unbalanced diet (insufficient animal proteins in proportion to carbohydrates) as for lack of calories. However, each production unit—usually the nuclear family—can subsist without consuming everything it produces. Certainly the standard of living is much lower than in an industrial society, but surplus is measured in a society with reference to the level of consumption of most of its members, not with reference to an outside group. The transition from forest agriculture to savanna agriculture marks the crossing of the threshold between bare subsistence and a surplus. This surplus is especially significant because it may consist of cereals and leguminous crops. Root crops are grown too, but while they constitute the important food product in the forest clearings, the proportion is reversed in the savanna. Now, cereals—sorghum, maize, rice and various kinds of millet—and leguminous crops—peas, beans, green and other—can be kept almost indefinitely, are easy to transport and to measure, and are uniform enough to be compared. These characteristics make possible some accumulation of a very fluid form of wealth. Thus the surplus may very easily be taken away from the producer, passed from hand to hand, and built into quite large concentrations.

The precious surplus is kept in granaries. The granaries are very conspicuous in savanna villages. Built very close to the houses but apart from them, they are huge baskets of clay-covered wattle, supported on a wooden platform so that they do not touch the ground. This protects their contents from the damp and from the depredations of small animals. The number and size of the granaries indicate the wealth of their owners. The relative wealth of each nuclear family can be ascertained at a glance. This shows that there are rich and poor people in a village; there is no longer the equality of the hunting band or the forest village.

Some granaries are obviously bigger and fuller than the others; these belong to the chief. Does he work harder than the others? Does he own larger fields? No, he receives part of the produce of the other men of the village, that is, he concentrates in his hands most, if not all, of the surplus produced by the other villagers. Of course, this wealth is not collected for his personal consumption; though he always eats his fill, the chief eats the same food as his subjects. But his granaries enable him to devote his whole time to governing, to supporting certain specialists, such as craftsmen, and, above all, a retinue of advisers and executive agents who make his power effective by sanctioning it, if necessary, by force. His granaries are also used as a reserve for public feasts and for periods of scarcity. Because one man has at his disposal the surplus produce of his community, he has the means of applying force and coercion, that is, political power, and this power enables him to appropriate the extra produce of other farmers. In this way the spiral of alternating and cumulative growth of income and power can continue.

This pattern, which we have described only in outline—habitat and techniques allowing production of an agricultural surplus, control of the surplus of a group by one of the members of the group, emergence and development of political power, reinforcement of the power to appropriate surplus produce—occurred thousands of times in the vast area which extends south of the equatorial belt, from the Atlantic Ocean to the Indian Ocean. This is the origin of chiefdoms, which are much more characteristic of precolonial Africa than forest villages or hunters' camps. Unlike the civilizations of the bow and of the clearings, the civilization of the granaries is not really marginal: a very high proportion of Africans have lived in savanna chiefdoms.

Of course there are many variations on this basic pattern, and it has led to various developments. Some chiefdoms are limited to a few villages or even to one, while others—the majority—have engaged in a process of struggle for domination in which they could only win or lose, submit or be conquered, but not remain independent. In this way kingdoms were built up, which could be centralized or federal. We are just beginning, with some difficulty, to construct their history, for there are few of the usual materials with which historians reconstruct the past (archives and monuments) south of the equator. Fortunately oral traditions, often very old and accurately memorized, exist where there has been a succession of sovereigns. When they have been collected in time, these traditions constitute documents of great value for the historian.

Thus Luba traditions open perspectives on the past of several kingdoms of the region which is now north-east of Angola, south of Congo (Kinshasa) as well as in Zambia. These traditions are confirmed by recent archaeological discoveries.

In 1957, Nenquin and Hiernaux discovered on the shores of Lake Kisale, not far from Manono in the north of Katanga Province, an immense cemetery, in which the dead were buried with pottery, jewelry and copper objects in the shape of a small "x" known as *Katanga croisettes*, which were for a long time used as money. These discoveries, together with what we know from Luba tribal traditions, tell us of a kingdom—or rather several kingdoms—whose origin goes back to a period contemporary with the European Middle Ages.

The first kingdom of this Lake Kisale region was inhabited by Luba, but the rulers belonged to another people, the Songe, who are now in the east of Kasai Province. After they had freed themselves from Songe domination, the Luba in their turn founded what some historians call the Luba Second Empire, which extended its influence over a large part of present-day Katanga. The Luba brought the institution of monarchy and their organizational techniques to their neighbors the Lunda, who, in their turn, founded in the seventeenth century a vast empire extending from the Kwango to Lake Moëro. In addition, the Lunda subjugated the kingdoms of the Bemba and the Rotse (now in Rhodesia), the chiefdoms of the Ovibundu (now in Angola) and several other small states in the Kwango region.

The prevailing rule of succession in the Luba kingdoms was patrilineal, and seems to have entailed many fratricidal quarrels. The kingdom became increasingly weak until the Chokwe invasion, towards the end of the nineteenth century. The Lunda have a matrilineal system in the south, but a patrilineal one in the north, perhaps due to Luba influence.

These few historical notes show up the part played by conquest in the savanna kingdoms and chiefdoms. The habitat facilitated military campaigns and population movements; the existence of a surplus which could be appropriated in the form of seasonal tribute was a strong incentive for the chiefs. To make the effort to build a great state makes no sense unless the subjects can provide revenue for the rulers; even if there were not such serious obstacles to penetrating into the forest, what would be the use of building a state by uniting villages which can subsist only by consuming everything they produce?

In the great kingdoms, where the chief's power is manifested to its fullest extent the foundations of his authority are clearly very different from those of lineage patriarch. And even in modest chiefdoms, this difference also exists, even though it is less obvious. According to Audrey I. Richards, for whom the chiefdom is "the dominant institution of the Bemba," the power of each chief rests on a fourfold base: his wealth, his retinue, his jurisdiction, his magical powers. The true wealth of a chief consisted of the number of his villages which supplied workers for his fields and young men for his army. He had also slaves taken in war or handed over as compensation for some crime, and he had a monopoly of ivory and elephant meat. The ownership of ivory enabled him to obtain through the Arabs, at the end of the nineteenth century, guns and trade goods, and thus to increase his power considerably.

The chief's retinue was composed of officials, his kinsmen above a certain rank, and other courtiers motivated by the hope of various advantages. Some of these followers commanded bands of warriors who seized surrounding districts, occupied them and exacted tribute from them; others arrested criminals, executed punishments by mutilation, collected taxes and supervised the carrying out of services required by authority.

The chief handed out justice in the first instance, while the High Chief presided over a court which acted as a court of final appeal, and it alone could administer ordeal by poison.

Because he inherited the name and guardian spirits of a dead chief, the chief had strong magical powers, which enabled him to influence the prosperity of his chiefdom. The state of his health affected the well-being of his subjects, his sexual life was of public importance and for this reason it was confined within the narrow limits of many prohibitions. In addition to this general influence, the chief could invoke the guardian spirits in the sacred enclosures where various relics were kept, especially the stools which are said to have been brought by the Bemba First Chief when he came from the Luba country.

Thus in a Bemba chiefdom the chief's authority was very different from the power exercised by a patriarch in a forest village. In the latter, authority over members of a lineage and those who have been assimilated into it belongs to the oldest man, who represents the common ancestor; it is a paternal authority, does not resort to obligation by force, and does not demand tribute for the profit of the patriarch. Indeed, he is not a rich man who can afford to live without working the land; between his and the other descendants of the ancestor, there does not exist that "moral distance which marks the establishment of sacred power" as de Heusch expresses it. A Bemba chiefdom was a state in miniature, since it displayed the essential characteristic of the state: a permanent organization with coercive powers.

The Bemba chiefdoms were organized amongst themselves. One of the chiefs—whom we call here the First Chief, the *Citimukulu*—ruled his own chiefdom, which was in the middle of the region, but he had also a certain pre-eminence over the other chiefs, although the latter were not his subordinates in a hierarchy. He owned this position to the fact that he could trace his descent in the matrilineal line back to an ancestress through more than twenty-five holders of the title. The retinue of the First Chief comprised from thirty to forty hereditary officials; to each of these was entrusted a secret ritual duty, such as the custody of relics or the performance of certain ceremonies. This political structure was not so much a unified state as a federation of states brought together under the supremacy of the chief of one of the state-chiefdoms.

The Lozi Unitary State

In other savanna societies, the political organization consists not of the union of chiefdoms but of a unitary state: a chiefdom has become a kingdom. The power of the chief-king is very high, the chief's retinue is a court with many dignitaries ranged according to complicated rules of precedence, and an administration of district officials who govern the various regions in the name of the king. Thus according to Max Gluckman, among the Lozi, who live in the Zambezi Valley, in Zambia, royalty, nationality and territory are considered as coincidental units, though in the Lozi language they correspond to different concepts. When the king's council sits as a court of justice, the place where each dignitary must sit in the wide courtyard which surrounds the royal dais is a spatial representation of the complexity of ranks and duties. On the king's right, the most important councillors sit on mats; these are the *induna*, who comprise two groups, the elders and the juniors; to the left are other councillors of lesser rank, the *likombwa*, who are also divided into elders and juniors; beside them, the mat which is called royal is reserved for the princes and the husbands of princesses, who are there to represent their wives. At a council meeting in 1942, Gluckman mentions forty-six *induna* to the right of the king, ranked according to the order of precedence of their titles, and, to the left, forty *likombwa* and princes. Each states his opinion according to his rank, in ascending order.

Among the Lozi, revenue from taxation, by means of which the state appropriates a fairly large amount of its subjects' surplus production, is shared ritually among the various rulers according to their rank. When the tribute was brought to the capital, a preliminary amount was taken out during the night for the reigning king. In the morning, in the presence of the people, he took out a second portion. Then shares were sent to the priests of various shrines, to the senior *induna*, and to the various councillors, according to their rank.

Rulers and Subjects among the Kuba

The existence of a savanna state, especially when it has a large number of dignitaries and officials, creates a division of society into two main groups, one above the other: the rulers, that is, not only those who have power to make decisions, but all those whose income is derived from taxes, and the ruled, that is, all those who give up part of their agricultural surplus to the former. The rulers' privileges are tied in with their offices, so they try to make these offices hereditary. Thus a class of nobles is formed. This social phenomenon may be clearly observed in the Kuba.

According to Jan Vansina, Kuba political organization may be described as a union of chiefdoms that acknowledge the supremacy of the chief of the Mbala, the *Nyimi,* to whom they pay tribute. The most important rulers are the chiefs who have the right to wear an eagle feather; these chiefs live in the royal capital, own a privileged estate, and their offices belong to a kinship group in the sense that only certain lineages have the right to elect an eagle-feather chief. The overwhelming influence of these men at court of course assures the electoral lineages of important advantages in nominating people to important offices. Thus an aristocracy is gradually built up; it is a hereditary group to which one must belong in order to achieve government office.

Msiri, the Adventurer

Recurrent migrations, and the rapid formation and sudden disappearance of kingdoms make difficulties for the historian of this part of Africa. The establishment by Msiri of the Yeke chiefdom (in what is now Katanga Province) may throw light on this process, since it occurred recently and is relatively well known. Msiri, the son of an ivory trader, was born about 1830 in Sumbwa (now in Tanzania). As his father's agent he visited the Katanga chief who was exploiting copper deposits (in the area of the present-day settlement of Jadotville). He installed himself there with a caravan, strongly armed with muskets obtained from the Arabs, which he put at the service of the Katanga chief, who was at that time at war with another chief, Pande. By taking advantage of their differences, maneuvering skillfully between the chiefdoms of the area, sending for Sumbwa men and making them marry women of the local groups, he succeeded in making himself master of a certain territory, took the name of Msiri, had himself proclaimed king, and called his kingdom Garengaze, the name of an aristocratic tribe of his home country. Drawing from Sumbwa symbolism, he invented a ritual based on the *kilungu* emblem (a shell) and human blood. He chose a capital, Bunkeya, which was to become a city of 12,000 or 15,000 inhabitants, bustling with the ceaseless coming and going of caravans, returning military expeditions, and markets. He divided this capital into sections, each headed by one of his favorite concubines.

With this city as its center, he organized the kingdom. The various chiefdoms which were compelled to recognize the supremacy of Bunkeya were not changed, but in each of them he placed a resident whose duties were to watch over the local chiefs and collect tribute. This resident, who could be a woman, had a band of warriors at his or her disposal.

Another source of Msiri's income was a huge commercial organization. Actually he kept up relations with the Arabs established in the Lake Tanganyika area and extended trade as far as Lake Nyasa, where Arabs from Mozambique had set up a depot on the road to Kilwa, their Indian Ocean port. He sold them ivory, slaves, copper and salt in exchange for guns, gunpowder, cloth and pearls. Wishing to extend his trade westwards, he sent his brother with a caravan to make connection with the Portuguese traders of Angola. His contacts became regular, and thus he achieved a commercial connection *de Angola a contra costa*, which, until then, had been effected only occasionally by a few Portuguese adventurers, the Pombeiros.

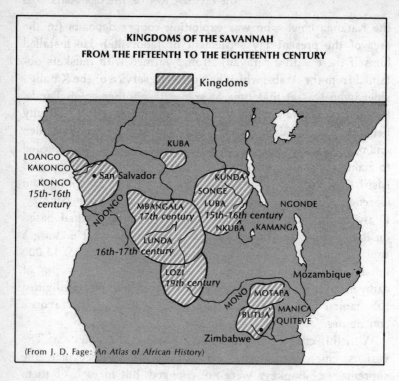

KINGDOMS OF THE SAVANNAH

FROM THE FIFTEENTH TO THE EIGHTEENTH CENTURY

///// Kingdoms

LOANGO
KAKONGO
KONGO
15th–16th
century
San Salvador
NDONGO
KUBA
MBANGALA
17th century
LUNDA
16th–17th century
KUNDA
SONGE
LUBA
15th–16th century
NKUBA
KAMANGA
NGONDE
LOZI
19th century
MONO
MOTAPA
BUTUA
MANICA
QUITEVE
Mozambique
Zimbabwe

(From J. D. Fage: *An Atlas of African History*)

Msiri died in 1891, killed by a Belgian officer during a skirmish with troops of the Congo Free State. Thus in about thirty years a small group of Sumbwa had established more than six hundred miles from their home country a well-organized kingdom which ruled over many chiefdoms and created a transcontinental trade route. Though Msiri's kingdom was already declining at the time of his death, it has lasted to the present day. The chief of the Yeke is a descendant of Msiri, and still lives in the large village of Bunkeya.

The Kingdom of Kongo and the West

Such trade routes across Africa south of the equatorial forest were certainly not the first. But we must not exaggerate the importance of the penetration of men from the outside world into the central regions of the continent; it was only occasional. On the west coast, the kingdom of Kongo is an exceptional case from the point of view of contacts between an African culture and a European culture.

When in 1482 the Portuguese reached the mouth of the River Zaire (later called the Congo) the kingdom of the Kongo had already passed its prime. Its capital, Mbanza Kongo, at the center of the kingdom, controlled six provinces, which were situated between the sea, the Zaire, the Bengo and the Kwango. But it seems very likely that it had once been very much larger, including also the kingdoms of Loango, Kagongo, Ngongo, and Matamba.

The monarchy was not hereditary, but the king's successor was most often one of his sons, although kinship was reckoned matrilineally. Although in theory he was an absolute monarch, the king had to take account of his nobles, and especially the provincial governors, who collected the taxes. Trade relations were facilitated by the existence of objects which fulfilled some of the functions of currency: cowries (small shells from the island of Luanda) and pieces of raffia cloth. The cowries and cloth had a scarcity value, which was the same for all individual pieces of the same category; they could easily be transported and accumulated. This was a rich kingdom; there were many blacksmiths who worked iron and copper, and many potters and weavers.

The first Portuguese who came were traders and missionaries, and seem to have been welcomed. After a violent but brief opposition by the nobility, the kings adopted the Catholic religion. Alfonso I, the greatest king of the Kongo, spread this religion throughout his kingdom, and did his best to adopt the European way of life, helped by the fact that Portuguese missions included blacksmiths, masons, farmers, and even two German printers who arrived in 1492. Young noblemen were sent to study in Lisbon, an embassy to the Papacy was established, a Congolese bishop was ordained as early as 1521, the government was modeled on Portuguese organization, and the capital was named San Salvador. The kings of the Kongo were treated more as allies than as vassals of the kings of Portugal.

This experiment in acculturation did not fulfill its promise. As stated by C. R. Boxer, the Portuguese, preoccupied with their great enterprises in India, Morocco and later in Brazil, lost interest in the Kongo and did not send the technical aid so frequently and so urgently demanded by the kings. Besides this, relations with the Portuguese settlers deteriorated: there were conflicts of interest with the traders, and later the slave traffic for the plantations in America. In 1510 the king of Portugal ordered Africans to be sent to the West Indies, noting that "one of these Negroes does as much work as four Indians." Strife, troubles, and periods of anarchy became frequent in the Kongo, and Pedro V, who reigned from 1859 to 1891, was no more than a district chief.

Matrilineal Kinship among the Peasants

The daily life of the peasants who live in the savanna kingdoms and chiefdoms is less spectacular, less comfortable, but also less dangerous, than that of their rulers. Its rhythm is set by the rainy seasons, which are always looked forward to, for they bring fertility to the fields. The important times in the annual cycle of farming communities are marked by sacred rituals for rainfall and for harvest. In some regions work must be concentrated in a rather short period, since the rest of the year is unsuitable for work in the fields. Thus the Bemba have only about four months of farm work in the year. This makes it necessary for them to build up reserves of grain and leguminous foods to feed the people for two-thirds of the year and to provide for the next sowing. Holding a surplus is not the only use of the granaries.

Although, unlike the situation in the forest, the kinship principle is not the base of all social relationships, especially those of authority, it regulates interpersonal relationships in private life just as much: kinship roles are exactly prescribed, and the lineages are still cooperative groups. In many savanna societies descent is reckoned in the female line.

A matrilineal system is not simply the mirror image of a patrilineal system. In a matrilineal system a couple's children belong to the lineage of their mother, not to that of their father. However, this does not mean that the mother has the rights of the lineage over them in the same way that children in a patri-lineal system are subject to the authority of their father as representative of the patrilineal lineage. Authority over a couple's children belongs to their mother's brother. It is the maternal uncle who receives the bride price when his nieces marry, and it is he who supplies it when his nephews take wives. However, since the father lives with his wife and children, at least when the children are young, he must exercise a certain amount of authority over them at home. Audrey Richards reports that among the Bemba, children are sent at the age of three to be brought up by their maternal grandmother, and as they grow up they are subjected more and more strictly to the authority of their maternal uncle. However, the father still has certain rights over his children: he is consulted about the marriages of his daughters, his son-in-law must work for him, and his children are free to visit him often. This divided authority over children cannot fail to build up tension between the father and his brother-in-law.

Succession goes in the maternal line. In the case of a Bemba chief, his office passes first to his brothers, then to his sisters' sons, and then to the sons of his sisters' daughters. The same applies to the position of an ordinary peasant: his name, his guardian spirit, his social status and obligations are taken over by his matrilineal heirs.

A matrilineal system does not imply a matriarchy, or govern-ment by women. It does not even necessarily mean that in a society with matrilineal descent a woman may claim superior status. When marriage is virilocal, as with the Kongo, the young wife lives with her husband's matrilineal group. The group of people who live together in a village is then composed of brothers, sons of the same mother (who herself lives elsewhere, with her husband who belongs to another matrilineage), their maternal uncle and his wife, their wives, their sisters' sons and unmarried daughters. It may thus be seen that the wives of brothers are isolated from their various kinship groups and live in their husbands' groups, away from their own children. It is not surprising that in this group of strangers they do not enjoy a specially high position, although they form by their lineage the essential chain which assures the transmission of status and property.

When residence is uxorilocal, as with the Bemba or the Yao, the position of women may be better. J. Clyde Mitchell states that in the Yao chiefdoms (in modern Malawi) the typical village consists of a nucleus of sisters gathered around their mother, the sisters' husbands, daughters and unmarried sons. Among the Bemba the lesser role of the husband is reflected in their idea of conception: the man only awakens the fetus, which is taken possession of by the guardian spirit of an ancestor entering into the womb of the pregnant woman.

Man in the World for the Luba

Analysis of the techniques, the economic system, the political and family institutions of a society may enable us to sketch some broad features of that society's vision of man and the world. But such general inferences must be confirmed and filled out by the rituals, beliefs and myths of that society, and "recognized" by those who practise them. It is for them to decide in the last instance whether the view of the world which is attributed to them really corresponds to their deep beliefs. We owe to Placide Tempels an insight into Luba philosophy.

For the Luba, the reality of everything, which is also the supreme value, is life, the vital force. For a European, energy is an attribute of being, but for a Luba it "is not an accident, it is even much more than a necessary accident, it is the very essence of being within the self. It is the being as it is, in its real wholeness, realized in its present existence, and capable of more intense realization. Being is that which possesses force." The fundamental principle of *being is energy* is the key to the Luba representation of the world. All beings—spirits of the ancient ones, living men, animals and plants—are immediately experienced as forces and not as static entities. The latter exist or do not exist, but they cannot be more or less intense, while being-forces may exist in greater or lesser degree. Continually influencing each other, their vital power is constantly varying.

This idea of existence rules the domain of human behavior. In all circumstances one must grow—growth is goodness—and avoid the only evil that exists—to become less. Invocations to the great ancestors are aimed at increasing vital energy; by entering into communion with them—their vitality is manifested by the incalculable number of their descendants—one becomes strong. People seek the intervention of diviners and magicians, who capture and master the forces which escape ordinary men because they know the words which strengthen life. When a person is ill, he expects of a cure not a localized therapeutic effect, but the strengthening of his whole being. The reason why so much importance is given by the Luba and other peoples to sexual vigor in men and fertility in women, as is shown by ritual and sculpture, is that procreation is obviously the most tangible expression of the growth of life. As with the Bemba, it is because of this constant communication between the vital forces which act upon each other that the sexual power of chiefs and kings often concerns the prosperity of the country and the fertility of its women and its fields.

The *muntu*—which should be translated as "person" rather than "man"—may grow ontologically, but may also diminish to the point of total disappearance. "the ultimate diminution of the being, the state into which some dead persons fall when they no longer have the means to make contact with beings living on the earth, and can no longer exercise their vital influence either for or against the strengthening of life." Death is a diminished state, but the living descendants of a dead man can, by means of their faithful offerings, transmit something of life to him; when the living are neglectful, the dead remind them of their duties by sending them illnesses or other troubles. But if one has no descendants, one is condemned to this final degradation, a kind of second death, this time total death.

An individual is defined by his name; he *is* his name. This is an inside name which is never lost, and is distinguished from the second name given on the occasion of an increase of strength, such as the circumcision name, the chief's name received at investiture, or the diviner's name received upon his possession by a spirit. The inside name is the indicator of a person's individuality within his lineage. For no man is isolated: he "constitutes a link in the chain of vital forces, a living link, both active and passive, fastened by the top to the link of his ascending line, and supporting at the bottom the line of his descent."

Traditional respect expressed to the chief of Bun Keya, Congo-Kinshasa

Tutsi King and Catholic missionary, Rwanda

African dance (traditional style), First World Festival of the Negro Arts,
Dakar, 1966

A Catholic priest celebrating the mass

Nigerian market, Ibadan

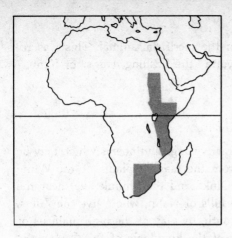

THE CIVILIZATION
OF THE SPEAR

"We brandish our spears, which is the symbol of our courageous and fighting spirit, never to retreat or abandon our hope, or run away from our comrades. If ever we shall make a decision, nothing will change us; and even if the heaven should hold over us a threat to fall and crush us, we shall take our spears and prop it. And if there seems to be a unity between the heaven and the earth to destroy us, we shall sink the bottom part of our spear on the earth, preventing them from uniting; thus keeping the two entities, the earth and the sky, though together, apart. Our faith and our decision never changing shall act as balance."

Thus sang the Gikuyu warriors when, at the end of the circumcision ceremony, the new fighter was given the weapons spattered with the blood of the sacrificial animal. This was reported to us by Jomo Kenyatta "the flashing dagger of Kenya" in 1938.

Poetry, Song and Decoration

The spear was glorified in many songs and poems which may be collected in East Africa, from the marshy plains of the White Nile where the Nuer, the Dinka and the Shilluk live, near the tenth parallel north, to the hills of Natal, where live the Zulus, near the thirtieth parallel south, by way of the high plateaus of the Great Lakes, the home of the kingdoms of the Ganda, the Nyoro, the Rwanda, near the equator (see map on preceding page). This huge area is not in one block; it is interrupted, particularly by the broad savanna zone of the civilization of the granaries, which, to the south of the high plateaus, extends as far as the Indian Ocean, approximately from Lake Nyasa to the River Limpopo. Because statues and masks are very rare in East Africa, this region has been said to be artistically poor. But this is to ignore its literature, its music and its delight in ornamentation.

Although convention permits us to speak of the literature of non-literate people, the term "the art of speech" is less paradoxical and serves better to suggest the importance of verbal expression in historical recitations and war poems or love poems. These are declaimed at feasts to commemorate military victories, in ceremonies at which the noble deeds of ancestors of the reigning dynasty are recalled and at night watches when the young warriors arouse their fighting spirit by telling the story of the heroes whom they hope to emulate.

The talent of the reciter is appreciated; this consists of rendering a set text in expressive manner as well as of improvising. In particular, historical poems, which legitimize the power of the rulers, are preserved by certain dignitaries who have to hand down from father to son without changing a word; sometimes their origin is so far back that they are expressed in an archaic language.

Ancient texts also serve as models for composing new songs of praise or defiance. This task is not reserved for specialists in rhetoric; the warriors themselves must create short poems to declaim before their comrades. The following poem, which is sung, was composed at the end of the nineteenth century. Rwanda warriors, starting out on an expedition, request the help of the king:

> The heroes are called to arms.
> A Mulima man invokes King Musinga.
> Listen to these Heroes;
> They are going into battle.
> Are you not also brave?
> They all set out, armed with bows and spears.
> You are brave in battle, we know.
> The heroes will pursue those who flee.
> They will attack the enemy fiercely.

The attention to the beauty of the verbal form, which is displayed as much in living poetry as in the set texts, and the accomplished poetry which is revealed even in translation, show clearly that in warlike societies literary skills are well developed.

The same is true of music. According to Alan P. Merriam, the area of civilization dealt with here is also an area of musical culture. It is especially characterized by the particular role of percussion instruments which are often played solo, while singing is accompanied by string instruments such as the zither and the musical bow. This invalidates the generally accepted notion that African music is dominated by rhythm marked by drums. In the Great Lakes region especially, choirs of women sing tender lullabies and melancholy love songs.

Weapons are decorated: spear points, swords, sheaths, quivers and shields are covered with nonfigural designs engraved in the iron, carved on wood, painted on leather. The Zulu warriors' equipment was a brilliant panoply, its beauty designed to enhance military prestige and to impress the enemy. Geometrical decoration is also found in beadwork and especially in basketry.

The motifs are traditional and have a meaning which throws light on the cultural values of the group. Basketry is the work of women, and some very fine miniature baskets are made only as gifts and to demonstrate the craftsmanship of the weaver.

In this region, whose northern and southern limits are more than three thousand miles apart, these arts appear in many varied styles. However, certain characteristics recur oftener than others: decoration favors quiet linear motifs and avoids over-elaboration; the material is not opulent, but very simple; the loud, full sound of drums and choral singing is often replaced by the voice of a solo singer accompanied by one zither or a melody played on a flute; poetry must be close-textured and concise; eloquence must not be enhanced by gestures. This complex of qualities has more than once been expressed by the adjective "aristocratic."

Aristocratic Values and Warrior Societies

Can this term be applied also to the societies in which such artistic forms have developed? On the level of the value system, an aristocratic society evokes the image of a group which gives prime importance to the virtues by which the individual stands out: personal courage, self-confidence, pride; a clear, strong sense of the collective superiority of his own group and a quiet scorn for other groups; a strong interest in marking the distance between himself and others by cultivating distinctive qualities. On the political level, to which it originally belongs, the term "aristocracy" is applied to government by a minority which in some way claims to have a hereditary right to rule.

Many East African societies have an aristocratic political structure, and even more have an aristocratic values system. Thus in Ankole, a Great Lakes kingdom, power is in the hands of the Hima pastoralists who constitute about one-tenth of the population, the rest of which is composed of Iru cultivators. The Luo, during their migrations in the Bahr el Ghazal, did not have an aristocratic government, but their social values were aristocratic. The underlying reason is that all these were warrior groups, and in the kind of fighting they practised—usually swift raiding expeditions—initiative, aggressiveness, individual courage, the knowledge of one's own superiority, were qualities essential for success.

War was not a cause of social upset, or a crisis; it was a period of intensified living, a phenomenon which was institutionalized and integrated into the economic and political organization. Thus among the Masai, who live in Kenya and Tanzania in the Kilimanjaro area, when the members of a band of warriors planned a raiding expedition, they asked the local chief to lay out a plan of attack and eventually to obtain the cooperation of other bands. Then, according to the description of G. W. B. Huntingford, the leaders of the expedition went to the diviner to get his authorization. This was not granted unless the diviner judged the circumstances propitious. When consent was given, the warriors prepared themselves by feasting on meat; scouts were sent out, and the expedition began. Expeditions were carried out against the neighboring tribes, and sometimes went as far as the coast, more than 250 miles away. Their object was the seizure of cattle, which upon the warriors' return, were shared according to very precise rules: a certain number of animals went to the diviner and to the warriors who had distinguished themselves; the rest were shared among the members of the expedition. If there were not enough cattle to distribute equably, the warriors divided themselves into two groups and fought for the booty. The members of the raided group were not enslaved or taken prisoner. The men who resisted during the battle were killed, and sometimes a warrior would carry off a woman to marry or a child to adopt.

These expeditions did not result in the loss of many human lives. The same was true when large Masai armies fought among themselves. The first European to cross Masai country, J. Thompson, reports that in 1883 he saw two enemy armies, each of about 3000 warriors, camped not far from each other. Only two detachments of selected men from each camp actually took part in the battle; their wives helped in the fighting and screamed encouragement to them; the winners took the losers' cattle.

The Gikuyu, neighbors of the Masai, were often victims of armed raids, but they too organized raids. According to Jomo Kenyatta, himself a Gikuyu, these expeditions occurred when a group of a few villages was threatened by a shortage of meat or milk because its own cattle had been reduced by an epidemic. The raiders tried to seize cattle without fighting by capturing them by surprise when they were away from the villages.

Still, for the Gikuyu, just as for the other peoples of the spear, war was the focus of the young men's passionate concern. The ideal type of the prestigious man was the victorious warrior. With his glittering weapons, multicolored shields, ostrich-feather head-dresses and the insignia of his military valor, painted in brilliant color on his body, he would tell of the feats he had accomplished and become giddy with the praises of his comrades.

Chaka

Warfare was also a matter of discipline and organization. It was the Zulus who developed these qualities to the highest degree of elaboration, through the energy and intelligence of one man, Chaka. Son of a Nguni chief, Chaka was born about 1790. He left his family when he was young and enlisted in the service of another chief, more important than his father, who gave him a good basic military education. When his father died, he managed to succeed him after killing a half-brother who had been named as heir by his father.

Chaka began by changing the weaponry, replacing the long-handled throwing spears, which often missed their aim and were then lost, with short-handled, wide-bladed assegais, which were to be used only by striking directly with the point. Warriors who disobeyed this order and returned from battle without their assegais were executed. Chaka also abolished sandals, which he thought slowed down the movements of the fighters. He organized the army into regiments of about a thousand men each. The total strength of the army has been estimated at fourteen or fifteen regiments. Each regiment lived in its own compound, had a special war cry, and a shield with distinctive colors. The warriors underwent a strict training and were not allowed to marry. Strategy too was modified by Chaka. According to Eileen J. Krige, he arranged his troops in four groups: two flanks and two central bodies, one behind the other. Executing a wheeling movement, one of the flanks would attack while the other hid, not coming into the battle until it was well under way; the forward central group, consisting of experienced fighters, would wait for the enemy to attack, while the rear central group would sit with their backs to the battle, forming a reserve.

Chaka had not built up such armies to carry out cattle raids; he was a conquering despot, and his many campaigns brought him into control of vast territories; he enlisted into his regiments the young men of the peoples he conquered, while the rest of the population was often massacred or driven away. But the Zulu wars as Chaka conducted them are exceptional in the civilization of the spear.

Why did warlike activities play a much more important part in this civilization than in the civilizations we have considered up to now? Perhaps we will be able to answer this question when we know more about the history of East African societies. At present we can only point out the conditions which have made the warlike development of these societies possible, desirable, and, in some cases, necessary. These conditions are on the technical and economic level.

Cattle as Capital

Nearly all the societies of the spear are pastoral; they belong to the "pastoral complex" culture area, to use Herskovits's expression once more. Now in Africa, cattle have an economic significance very different from that of land. Human labor expended on cattle has a much higher yield than when it is devoted to agricultural tasks; a few breeders and herdsmen are enough to produce from a fair-sized herd a large income in meat, leather, milk and blood. Though it is uncommon for groups to subsist entirely on the products of cattle-raising, some groups do so all the time. Thus the Hima nomads of north-west Rwanda bleed their animals to use the blood, which, with dairy products, constitutes their regular diet. Even with peoples who also practise agriculture, some categories of the population, such as young people between the ages of 15 and 20 among the Jie of Kenya, live exclusively on these animal foods during the long periods they spend in the grazing camps. Everywhere these foods are a last resort in case of necessity. If it is not consumed directly, produce from cattle may be used to obtain goods and services by exchange. Thus cattle in themselves constitute a true economic value, while land, which in traditional Africa is never in short supply, is of value only because of the labor which is expended on it. Every family can be sure of a plot to clear and plant; it cannot obtain possession of a herd by the same means. A herd can be collected without losing any of its value; it does not die out. On the other hand, there is no use in collecting land; if it is not worked its value is nil. In addition, cattle are movable goods, and do not require their owner to stay in one place; they may be moved without losing any of their value. Finally, since the importance of a herd can be measured by counting the heads of cattle, the value of several herds may be compared with some precision.

These few characteristics make cattle into true wealth, and enable them to play a role which recalls, though not very closely, that of capital in Western economic systems. The cattle-owner, like the capitalist, receives income without working, sees his income transformed into capital if he does not spend it, can at any time transfer it or exchange it for other goods. A society which has this "natural" capital—since these characteristics of cattle come to it, not from an economic system but from its own nature—has different possibilities, also different obligations, from those of an agricultural society.

Pastoral Mobility

This valuable and movable property may be easily lost and easily acquired. A pastoral society without means of defense would run a strong risk of being completely dispossessed. Farmers' harvests may also be taken by force and granaries may be robbed, but this booty consisting of consumer goods is less attractive than capital in the form of cattle. Thus it is not surprising that military organizations should be developed in pastoral societies, especially as pastoralists, less compelled to spend their whole time producing the necessities of daily living, have more leisure to train themselves in the profession of war and to practise all the activities associated with it: war dances, making of equipment, memorization and reciting of war poems. The herds do not graze in man-made pastures. Thus they depend for their food on what the natural habitat has to offer. In the Nile region, the habitat consists of marshy grasslands, seasonally flooded, in the Great Lakes region it is high, grassy savanna, which, in the dry season, provides no nourishment except in the valleys; further south there are hills covered with various kinds of vegetation, scanty in some areas, abundant in others. It is very seldom that a herd can feed throughout the year without covering considerable distances; it also happens that the annual rainfall pattern is disturbed by irregularities, which necessitate longer journeys than usual in search of pasture. These conditions oblige pastoral societies to be constantly on the move—sometimes the whole group travels, sometimes only some sections of it—and enables them to lead an entirely nomadic life. Nomadism, which pre-supposes living almost entirely by the direct consumption of pastoral produce, is a frugal, austere and free way of life, and its spirit is well expressed in the restraint of artistic forms.

Since they have to be constantly mobile, especially in the dry season when they must seek pastures and water holes, pastoral groups cannot be very large. This fact, together with the austerity of their life and the comradeship of warriors, favors social homogeneity of the group. E. E. Evans-Pritchard shows that the Nuer, who live in the south of the Sudan Republic, lack political organization on the state level. For these reasons, pastoral societies rarely show stratification into a ruler group and a ruled group.

Mixed Societies and Caste

The situation is very different in mixed societies which have resulted from an encounter between pastoralists and agriculturalists. An armed raid with the object of seizing cattle is a profitable operation; taking the stores of millet or beans from a village of agriculturalists is profitable only if the raiders are merely passing through the country. But when the fertility of a region already occupied by cultivators enables a group of pastoralists to settle there, the looting of agricultural products would be a very bad policy. So what happens in this case?

The Iru farmers of Ankole tell that at one time, in the beginning, the pastoralists lived in the east of the country and the agriculturalists in the west; they were each ruled by their own lineage chiefs, and they exchanged the products of their means of subsistence. It is to be feared that this idyllic harmony existed only in the imaginations of the Iru peasants, who are dreaming of a golden age when they were not exploited. Actually, when the East African pastoralists settled in farming country, they dominated the cultivators, who, having no fighting force strong enough to resist them, could not prevent them from settling. Also, wanting to gain possession of this very valuable commodity, cattle, they became dependent on the invaders. Thus the pastoralists were able without much difficulty to establish them-

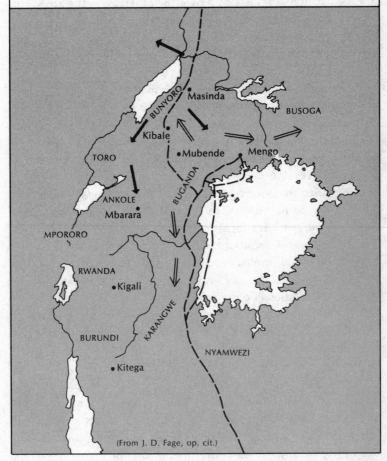

THE GREAT LAKES KINGDOMS
OF THE EIGHTEENTH AND NINETEENTH CENTURIES

⟹   Expansion of the Buganda in the nineteenth century

➡   Bunyoro renaissance 1870-1880

- - - -   Arab trade routes in the nineteenth century

BUNYORO

Masinda

BUSOGA

Kibale

TORO

Mubende

Mengo

BUGANDA

ANKOLE

Mbarara

MPORORO

RWANDA

Kigali

KARANGWE

BURUNDI

Kitega

NYAMWEZI

(From J. D. Fage, op. cit.)

selves as masters. They did this in Ankole, forming, as K. Oberg shows, a state encompassing pastoralists and agriculturalists. Each group had its own hereditary status, which offered unequal access to power and wealth.

The upper caste, the Hima, comprised pastoralists who were descendants of the conquerors; one of them, who belonged to one lineage which had set itself up over the others, was the king. The other cattle owners recognized his precedence by rendering homage to him as clients: they contracted to follow him in war and to give him periodically a certain number of head of cattle. In return, the king protected his clients in the case of raids directed against them and settled their quarrels.

The Iru cultivators were not allowed to own productive cows, only barren ones or male calves to be slaughtered for meat. Thus the Hima did not allow out of their possession the privileged goods which were the basis of their power; similarly they reserved for themselves the profession of war, and forbade the Iru to become warriors. Marriage between the castes was forbidden. The Iru had to pay tribute to the Hima chiefs who represented the king, and work for them without recompense when required. There are several variations on this main theme of the stratification of agriculturalists and pastoralists into two hierarchical hereditary groups. Thus in Rwanda, another mixed state next to Ankole, the relationship between pastoralists and agriculturalists has taken the form of a feudal regime in which a pastoralist would grant a cultivator possession of a cow while keeping for himself the ultimate ownership. Thus the cultivator could benefit from certain products—milk and male calves—of the animals he kept, while the pastoralist remained the owner, was able to take possession at any time, and obtained in return farm products and labor. This institution made it possible to create personal relationships of dependence on the one side and protection on the other, cutting across caste lines, which helped to maintain the solidarity of this stratified society.

It has been stated that in the pastoral area of East Africa cattle are of more importance in the ritual sphere and in the domain of social prestige than on the economic level. We hold the contrary opinion: that it is the economic value of cattle, together with war, which has become a center around which other cultural aspects have crystallized. It is true that in mixed (pastoral and agricultural) societies, and even in many semi-sedentary pastoral societies (in which agriculture is also carried on) farm products play a greater part in the daily diet than cattle products. In an industrial society too our subsistence comes from fields and herds, not from machines; yet the latter have much greater economic importance.

The "Favorite Bull" of the Longarim

The close association between these two cultural foci—war and cattle—appears strikingly in a strange institution of the Longarim, described by Andreas Kronenberg. Among these pastoralists, who live in the Province of Equatoria of the Sudan Republic, a young boy at the end of his puberty chooses a calf which will become his favorite animal. To tame it, he rubs its back with cow dung every day. Thus begins a long process of identification between the man and the animal. The identification will be more or less intense depending on whether or not the calf will one day be castrated. When it gets old, if it has been castrated, the ox is slaughtered and eaten by its "father" at a ritual meal with his age-mates, and is replaced. The favorite bull, which has not been castrated, is never killed, except on the tomb of its "father," and a man may have only one favorite bull in his lifetime. The man is often called by the name of his favorite bull, and in time his own name is forgotten. When a favorite bull fights with another animal, his "father" must kill the latter immediately, and when two favorite bulls fight the "fathers" must also fight. When the bull dies its "father" exposes himself to various dangers in the hunt or in battle; he must wear mourning as for the death of a close relative; he sometimes even commits suicide.

The identification of cattle and men often appears in the area of the civilization of the spear, but seldom in so individual a way as with the Longarim. The Dinka establish an analogy between the life of man and that of cattle, says Godfrey Lienhardt. Thus men imitate cattle. Holding up the bent arms to imitate horns is thought very elegant and is a common gesture in dances. In some dances, girls and boys indulge in a highly stylized imitation of the behavior of cows and bulls. In Rwanda the wives of big chiefs wear copper ornaments which suggests horns and walk with a cow-like rhythm.

The Longarim think that a man's affection for his favorite bull inspires him to action. "When I see my favorite bull my heart opens and I am ready to start some undertaking." Such undertakings are those which require daring: organizing a raid, directing a leopard hunt.

To understand this institution fully, we must consider it in relation to two others, those of the best friend, and of age classes. Most of the Longarim have a best friend, chosen at adolescence from among age-mates. This friendship is validated by sacrifices. Each must watch over the other's interests more than over his own; he must keep nothing secret from his friend; they form a team in all dangers and support each other. Each has also his duties towards the other's favorite animal; he must give it a bell and the ivory ornament which is hung around the animal's neck. But above all, when dances, hunts and fights take place, he must praise his friend. Praise is very important to the Longarim, and it also encourages valorous action.

Age Class

The organization of age classes is a cultural institute characteristic of the civilization of the spear; it is found in the modern states of Sudan, Kenya, Tanzania and South Africa. It is a horizontal division of society which cuts across descent lines. Among the Longarim, a new age class is formed by the young men when they consider their number sufficient. Age-mates have many collective activities: ceremonies, hunts, dances, expeditions. His age-mates are the first to be informed of a "father's" choice of a favorite animal, and they will organize the first hunts in his honor. Thus the choice of a favorite animal concerns the whole age class: a man must have a favorite bull because "we need a strong man who helps his comrades in time of war" and "a man without a favorite bull is like a woman."

A Longarim man does not necessarily remain all his life in the same age class. If he has striking qualities or has accomplished certain feats, he may be promoted to a higher age class. Thus a man's success is determined by the age class to which he belongs and his prestige within that age class.

When Evans-Pritchard was carrying out his research among the Nuer, six age classes comprised living members, but the two oldest classes had only a few survivors. It is with reference to these categories that the position of every Nuer man is structurally defined in relation to every other man. Thus a man may not marry the daughter of an age-mate, because he is united to her father; the utmost equality prevails between all age-mates, and they have an attitude of respect towards the members of higher age classes.

Among the Gikuyu, the Masai and the Zulus, age classes have a primarily military function. A Zulu regiment is nothing but a group comprising all the men who are about the same age.

Age classes usually start out from initiation. The bonds that are created between all the boys who have been initiated together persist throughout their lives; age classes institutionalize these bonds.

Initiation

Initiation plays an important part in the whole of Black Africa. It is a rite of passage from childhood to adulthood, and much has been said about it as a painful ordeal. It is true that the most common initiation practices, circumcision and excision, are painful operations; the Nuer cut into the brow down to the bone in six long slashes from ear to ear; the scars remain for a lifetime, and it is even said that their traces can be seen on the skulls of dead men. But these mutilations are only part of a long liturgy which dramatizes a boy's or girl's accession to the responsibilities of adult life. Many Africans agree with Jomo Kenyatta that "the abolition of initiation would mean the disintegration of the tribe." To the Gikuyu, the Christian missionaries' prohibition of clitoridectomy and initiation appears as a threat of de-Africanization. So they reacted by setting up an independent school system. Chaka, however, did not hesitate to abolish circumcision, which did not seem to him to be essential to the intensive military training which he imposed on the young men. But this abolition was in an entirely different context: since it was not the object of foreign attempts at abolition, circumcision did not become for the Zulus a symbol of their threatened culture.

The initiation ritual is more than a painful surgical operation, and initiation itself is more than a ritual: it is education. While being prepared for the ceremonies, which may last for weeks or even months, the children live apart from their family home; the girls are entrusted to mature, experienced women, the boys to wise, respected men. The many things they have seen, the impressions they have received during their participation in family and village life, are summed up and explained. It is not a matter of transmitting esoteric knowledge or revealing mysteries, but of teaching correct behavior, explaining it and impressing it on the memory. Among the Pare, the Shamba and the Ngu, who live in Tanzania, next to the Masai, the instructors make the children learn a very short song, which has to be explained as its meaning is sometimes obscure, and they illustrate their lesson by showing a baked clay figurine which represents or suggests the approved or disapproved behavior. H. Cory has collected hundreds of figurines and the songs that go with them. The Shamba boys recite that "a cat will even steal to feed its young";

they will remember later that they must take care of their children. Or again: "The rhinoceros is proud of his horn, but it may cause him to die of thirst"; which means that one must not seek to stand out from others: the rhinoceros, proud of being distinguished from other animals by his one horn, cannot, because of this horn, reach the water at the bottom of deep holes during the dry season. Among the Pare, a statuette with big ears seems to be listening anxiously: it is the husband whose wife has just given birth and who doubts the paternity of the child; the advice to the Ngu boys is: "Keep calm if your wife has given birth to a child. What do you want to find out?"

In African education, stress is placed on interpersonal relations. It is of the highest importance that every person should know how to conduct himself towards other people. The ideal picture which is implied by this education and which more or less consciously inspires it, is that of a society of individuals well adapted to their various social roles, whose social relationships are therefore easy and harmonious. Even where warlike valor is glorified, education is not aimed at developing strong individual personalities which would not adjust well to the life of a community. This orientation is very close to some modern educational trends, which seek to set up situations which will form personalities well adapted to their social milieu.

Initiation has other functions than stating the position of young people who are reaching the age of adulthood. Among the Masai, before a boy could be circumcised his father must "cross the fence." After he had made mead and prepared his warrior's equipment, he spent four days alone in a little hut outside his compound; then the old men came to find him and told him to lay down his arms: he had become an old man. Among the Gikuyu the community was divided into two categories, *mwangi* and *maina*: one belonged to one or the other according to one's birth: if one generation was *mwangi* the following one, that of the sons, was *maina* and that of the grandsons was *mwangi* again. All the people who were *mwangi* (or *maina)* practised together the activities corresponding to the different stages of life: from eighteen to forty years of age a man was a warrior, then, at the same time he participated in government, then he reached old age, the age of wise counsel. A ceremony was held to mark the time when the government passed from the *mwangi* to the *maina* or vice versa. Thus youth, maturity and old age, which are stages of the individual's life in Western society, were integrated into a social order which was perhaps more efficient for the society and more satisfying for individuals.

Divine Kingship

The men of the spear and of the herd, groups of free and equal comrades, free from the servitude of sedentary farming, formed state societies with hierarchical castes in the agricultural regions where they settled. Their domination, based on military superiority and the exclusive ownership of wealth in the form of cattle, was supported by the labor of the agriculturalists. In these states, royalty took on a characteristic which has been called divine, sacred or despotic. This phenomenon is perhaps due to influences from the east, but the glorification of the king beyond common human nature also corresponded to a convention, if not to a political requirement: the justification of the concentration of privileges in the hands of one caste, which was close to being superhuman, since one of its members at least was the equal of the gods.

This divine kingship is characterized by a certain number of features which are found in various degrees in the societies of the Great Lakes region. The king is identified with his kingdom so closely that if his strength declines his country becomes weak; that is why he cannot survive the onset of old age; he lives in ritual isolation which as far as possible prevents contacts with the profane, he cannot eat in public, often during audiences he is protected by a curtain from the public gaze; theoretically his power is absolute, he is the master of the life and property of each of his subjects; the king is surrounded by dignitaries with specialized ritual functions, who form a large court. The queen-mother has a very important official position, considerable power, and is surrounded by her own court. This complex of features—not all of them have been mentioned—which are characteristic of divine kingship, enabled Roland Oliver to present an attractive hypothesis about the origin of the builders of Zimbabwe.

Zimbabwe

In 1871, Karl Mauch discovered, not far from the town of Victoria in Rhodesia, a whole complex of constructions in ruins, built of granite blocks cut roughly in the form of bricks; in one valley a wall about two miles long forming an elliptical enclosure inside which were other walls and a conical tower; on a hill, fortifications. The boldest hypotheses were put forward to account for the presence, which seemed so unusual in Africa, of Zimbabwe, "the house of stone."

It is now accepted that some parts of these structures were dated by the carbon 14 method to the sixth century A.D; that Zimbabwe was a fully active center until about the fifteenth century, since important objects have been found—Persian faiences, Chinese porcelain, Arab glasses—which date from the thirteenth, fourteenth and fifteenth centuries; and that in the sixteenth century, when the Portuguese were arriving in the area, the capital of the kingdom of the builders of Zimbabwe had been moved to the north, and another dynasty, the Rozwi, to whom we must attribute the construction of certain Zimbabwe buildings, were establishing themselves there.

The descendants of those who had emigrated to the north, known to the Portuguese by the name of Karanga, belonged to the Shona population. The king of this group, the Monomotapa, had made a strong impression on these Europeans, who described the protocol of his court. Now, according to this description, the Monomotapa displays the characteristics of divine kingship. According to Oliver, the parallel is especially striking between the Karanga on the one hand, the Ankole and the Rwanda on the other. Thus he concludes that we have sufficient basis to state: "The political and dynastic institutions of the Zimbabwe-Monomotapa culture and the Ankole-Rwanda culture must have a common origin."

If this is so, the massive structures of Zimbabwe—in any case there can be no doubt that they were built by Africans—constituted the last stage of the development of certain societies of the civilization of the spear, which had come a long way from their origins in the austere life of the pastoral warriors.

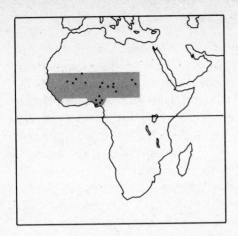

THE CIVILIZATION OF CITIES

An Idealist and Classical Art

These two adjectives, idealist and classical, suggest Greek sculpture of the fifth century B.C.: realistic faces, which are yet not portraits, a regard for anatomical proportions but features more regular and harmonious than in real life, a serene, intense expression. They are equally applicable to the pottery and bronze heads discovered in 1938 and 1957 at Ife in Nigeria, and dated about the twelfth or thirteenth century. At this time Ife was a city-state whose king, the *oni*, was recognized as the religious leader by the other Yoruba towns. For Ife is the place from which earth spread out on the original waters to form the world.

Odua, the divine ancestor of the various Yoruba dynasties, came down from heaven and set down on the surface of the waters a little earth and a hen; the hen scratched the earth and sent it out in different directions. Thus the world was created around Ife.

The perfect workmanship of these statues is extraordinary. The brass heads were made by the lost wax method, described by Leon Underwood (a sculptor who himself uses this technique) in his work on West African bronzes. A wax model, about a quarter of an inch thick, is first made, over a clay core if the finished object is to be hollow; in the upper part, according to the angle at which the model is set, a certain number of wax rods are fixed; the model is covered inside and out with wet, heat-resistant clay, the outer layer being very thick to make the whole thing very solid; if necessary it is built up further with iron points. When the clay is dry it is fired. This melts the wax model and leaves an empty space between the kernel and the covering, into which liquid metal is poured. At Ife the head was placed in such a way that the poured metal would spread over the face first, so that the delicate model would be more likely to be well formed, then air bubbles and broken bits of clay were removed through the channels left open at the back. When the metal has cooled, the outside mold and the kernel are broken. Faults in casting are rectified in the same way: the repair is first made in wax which is covered with clay and then melted and then replaced with molten metal.

This extremely skillful use of lost wax casting for large objects (the heads are life size) and this faithful representation of the visual impression of an idealized human type are so exceptional in African art, most of which expresses an intense subjective vision, that the question has been raised about the origin of Ife art. The origin of the Yoruba, according to the interpretation which may be applied to some of their traditions, is said to be between Egypt and Ethiopia, whence they are said to have arrived in the Ife area during the first millennium of the

Christian era. This origin, and the similarity between the diadem on certain Ife heads and the crown of the kings of Nubia are the basis of Denise Paulme's hypothesis which attributes Ife art to Nubian sources.

However, in that part of West Africa which was to become Nigeria, there exist older artistic traditions. William Fagg thinks that one of these, that of Nok, is not unrelated to Ife art. In 1943 a very large number of fragments of baked clay statues was discovered in the tin mines near the village of Nok on the Jos plateau. According to the carbon 14 method, they date from a period extending from 900 B.C. to 200 A.D. Like the Ife heads, the Nok heads are life-size; these are the only two examples in Africa of ceramic sculpture of such dimensions. The Nok faces are strongly modeled in a more "African" style, that is, reality is interpreted according to the intellectual and emotional conception of the artist and his group; but according to Fagg, the contrast between Nok and Ife is much less marked in the style of the bodies of the statues, which are simplified in both cases, probably for aesthetic reasons. Thus he concludes that we may consider Nok and Ife as two collateral branches which have grown out of an older civilization.

Another vanished culture of the area of the civilization with which we shall deal in this chapter is that of the Sao. A huge body of material, comprising several thousand pieces—pendants, rings and other bronze ornaments made by the lost wax method, iron instruments for hunting and fishing, human and animal figurines in baked clay—were brought to light by the excavations in Chad country by Annie and Jean-Paul Lebeuf. Lebeuf estimates that most of these objects were made by Sao people who settled in the country about the tenth and eleventh centuries; they founded there the walled cities of Midigué, Gawi and Tago. The Sao ceramic human figures are very crudely made; some are very expressive; the lips protrude, the mouth is very wide and half open, and they suggest, almost painfully, a scream or a cry for help; while the limbs are barely sketched in, certain details—

necklaces, tattooings— are shown so markedly that it sometimes seems that the artist has carved the figurine only to show off these ornaments. The metal objects, on the other hand, show very careful finishing.

A Massive, Flamboyant Art

Ife, Nok and Sao have been known only for a few decades. But at the end of the last century another astonishing body of art, that of Benin, in the Gulf of Guinea, was discovered. In 1897 an English vice-consul, accompanied by eight Europeans and two hundred and eighty porters decided to visit the king—the oba— of the town of Benin, with which Great Britain had concluded a treaty a few years previously. The oba had him informed that he was busy with sacrificial ceremonies and could not receive his visit. The vice-consul took no notice and about fifteen miles from the town his party was attacked and massacred: the only survivors were two Europeans and forty porters. Less than two months later a British punitive expedition captured Benin and found there a huge quantity of bronze pieces, ivory sculptures and other art objects. Many of these objects were taken to London and sold there. In this way Europe suddenly learned about Benin art, the most characteristic examples of which were bronze plaques representing military subjects; memorial heads supporting carved tusks; and ivory masks.

Unlike the artistic traditions which have been mentioned so far, Benin art belongs to a society which is still living, although it has long since passed its period of florescence. K. Onwonwu Dike has established that when the first Europeans, the Portuguese, arrived in 1485, the town of Benin held sway over several hundred villages occupied by the Bini, and was at the height of its power. According to traditions collected at this time, which are still to be found among the Bini, the first royal dynasty was connected with Ife. It comprised twelve oba, probably mythical, and ended with a rebellion which set up a republican regime. A new king, again from Ife, re-established the monarchy. Dike thinks that this event may have occurred in the twelfth century, for in 1485 the fifteenth *oba* was reigning. The present king is the thirty-fifth *oba*. For four centuries—from 1485 to 1897—the city-state of Benin remained independent and maintained constant commercial relations with the Portuguese, the Dutch, the French, the English, the Spanish, the Danes, and the Brandenburgers. These Europeans came to Benin for pepper, ivory, slaves and palm oil. This trade, closely controlled by the *oba*, was one of the principal sources of the prosperity of the city with seven gates.

According to Bini tradition, Oguola, the sixth *oba* of Benin, requested the *oni* of Ife to send him a metal-caster who would teach the Bini craftsmen how to smelt metal. This may have happened about 1280. Attempts have been made to trace from this time the temporal sequence of the various works known to us. Fagg interprets it as "a sort of counterpoint, an interaction between two styles, the tribal and the courtly." The "tribal" style is known to us only by a few wooden objects brought from Bini country in 1897: it is very rustic; the court style is represented by works in bronze and ivory. The metal casters were not allowed, under pain of death, to work for anybody other than the *oba*. The first heads, dating from the fourteenth and fifteenth centuries, are the closest to those of Ife, being naturalistic and representational. In the sixteenth and seventeenth centuries, the period of the plaques, objects were produced in greater quantity; copper was imported from Europe by sea, while previously it had come by caravan across the Sahara; the idealization of faces was replaced by stylization, and ornaments, especially the huge collars, took on a very great importance. Finally, from the eighteenth century on, there was a "flamboyant decadence": a stereotyped face, an overabundance of superficial decoration, with innumerable symbols of power, less technical skill. Without doubt, since the sixteenth century European influences affected Benin art, but in a way which does not seem to have changed its style directly. Many European soldiers are represented in bronze, small Portuguese heads decorate the crown of the admirable ivory mask in the British Museum, and, as Philip Dark points out, the wall plaque, an unusual form of art, seems to have been for the Bini a way of asserting themselves to the Europeans, by casting in bronze the memories of past *oba* and their glorious deeds, and the wars and ceremonies of the mighty city of Benin.

To the west of the Yoruba country, the town of Abomey, capital of the Kingdom of Dahomey, independent until it was conquered by France in 1893, was an especially powerful center in the seventeenth and eighteenth centuries, when, according to historians, the slave trade provided important revenues for the kings and enabled them to acquire arms. As at Benin, the crafts-men worked for the king. In the palace of Abomey, the bas-reliefs in unbaked mud recall great deeds by the dynasties and the warriors; brass figurines, cast by the lost wax method, suggest in anecdotal style scenes from the life of the aristocracy; iron pieces, like the amazing statue of Gu, god of war, the largest wrought-iron sculpture known in Africa, bear witness to a very lively inspiration.

The art of Kumasi, capital of the Ashanti kingdom, which was conquered by the English in 1895, is especially known for three types of objects: stools, "dolls" and weights for gold dust. The stools, as in many African societies, are insignia of power, granted by the king to those on whom he was conferring a high honor; the base of the stool is of wood carved in open work, with great stress on form. One of these stools, covered with gold leaf, was given by the heavenly powers to King Osai Tutu at the beginning of the eighteenth century; since then it has been the symbol of the power and unity of the Ashanti nation. The "dolls" are worn by pregnant women to assure them of beautiful chil-dren. Their unusual form—the face is a flat disk and the body is a very slightly modified cylinder—has suggested to Denise Paulme the hypothesis of an Egyptian origin—the New Kingdom mirrors, in copper, bronze and sometimes wood, have the same shape. To weight gold dust, the Ashanti use charming figurines of brass, made by the lost wax method, very varied in subject: fish, insects, plants, geometrical shapes. This diversity does not affect the accurate standardization of the weight of figurines which have the same name: only the chief has the right to use heavier weights than his subjects. The Agni, of the present-day Ivory Coast, also cast gold weights. Gold jewelry—masks and pendants—was also made by Kumasi craftsmen.

Cities of Exchange and Commerce

The artistic traditions of West Africa which we have described have produced objects very diverse in style. But they have only been able to develop in a socio-economic situation which was much the same for all of them, and different from that which was at the base of the other great African civilizations we have been considering. Here we have a new kind of civilization—that of cities.

The works of art we have mentioned are designated by names of towns—Sao cities, Ife, Benin, Abomey, Kumasi—and presuppose the existence of urban activities. Only a very specialized body of craftsmen can master the lost wax technique to make delicate gold jewelry, or work ivory as at Benin. Trade relations with distant countries are necessary to import the copper needed for smelted metals. There must be governments with incomes higher than those which can be produced by agricultural surplus so that such expenses can be met. But for the exchange and profit made possible by large-scale trading, the arts of West Africa could not have been what they were. And this large-scale trade could be carried on only between towns in which the natural produce of the hinterland and manufactured objects could be brought to a center for export, and where many imported goods were handled.

These commercial cities were not all in the Bight of Benin area, where the art centers we have mentioned were situated. From the coast of Senegal to Kordofan in the Sudanese savanna and the dry steppe which are on the southern edge of the Sahara, there were cities which, long before penetration by Europeans, were the termini of trans-Saharan caravans, centers of exchange, and capitals. The capital of Ghana, (on the site of Kumbi Saleh) the land of gold, had 30,000 inhabitants in the eleventh century; the name Mali, the city where lived the king of the empire of the same name, was used in turn for settlements on the sites of Jeriba, Mani-Kura, Niani and Kangaba; Timbuktu and Djenne were brilliant centers of intellectual life; the former, according to Jean Suret-Canale, functioned as a terminus for the trans-Saharan caravans, while the latter, in the interior, collected products of Sudanese origin and redistributed imported goods; Gao on the Niger, capital of the Songhai empire since the beginning of the eleventh century, had fifty thousand in the sixteenth century. Ouagadougou, capital of a Mossi state; the Hausa "seven cities": Daura, Kano, Rano, Zaria, Gober, Katsena, Biram; Ndjimi, capital of the princes of the Chad kingdom of Kanem; El Fasher at Darfur, where caravans from Chad, the eastern Sahara and the Nile all met: these centers bore witness to the large geographical area over which the civilization of cities extended.

The presence of many cities of exchange and commerce, which are very rare elsewhere in Africa, allows us to consider the immense region which extends from the Atlantic Ocean to the Nile Valley and from the Sahara to the equatorial and Atlantic forests or the coast of the Gulf of Guinea (where the Atlantic forest zone is interrupted), as characterized by one type of civilization, that of cities. The natural habitat of this zone is one of varied vegetation: savanna with deciduous trees, steppes with thorny trees and bushes, and, near the coast, heavily wooded regions. The climate consists of two clear-cut seasons, the dry season becoming longer and harsher the nearer one comes to the Sahara. Of course the whole population of this area was not urban; it is even likely that the peasants were much more numerous than the town-dwellers. However, the case is the same in many countries which are nevertheless considered as clearly urbanized. Thus in the decade 1930-40, the only country in which more than half the population lived in settlements of more than 5000 inhabitants was Great Britain (65.9%) followed by Germany (46.1%), the United States (42.3%), France (31.2%); in this list, which is taken from William Bascom, the Yoruba country occupies a very high place with an urbanization index of 37.4%. Whatever may have been the relative numerical importance of the population of the cities of the Sudan savanna and the Benin coast, it was the cities which gave the societies and cultures of this area their characteristic pattern. And the same is true for the peasant groups, for nearly all of them are linked to the towns by political, fiscal, commercial, religious and interpersonal relations.

It is no less true that, if the city is the major focus of the civilization to which this chapter is devoted, the peasant village is the secondary focus. Village culture has its own art, which we shall now consider.

Masks and Secret Societies

The kind of African art which has most impressed Westerners is perhaps the masks of the savannas—those of the Bambara, the Dogon, the Mossi, the Bobo, the Senufo and, on the borders of the savanna and the forest, the Bamum and the Bamileke. The object itself—the mask—is rare in the European artistic tradition, and its mysterious psychological profundity reaches down into deep and dark levels of personality.

These masks display so rich a variety of forms that it is very difficult to say what they have in common aesthetically. Sculptors have treated with great freedom such natural forms as the human face and animal heads; they aimed at the forceful expression of an emotional concept. Unlike statues, masks are not made to be gazed at while they are motionless in the calm light of day.

They exist only when they come out, usually at night; accompanied by music and singing, they dance in constant movement; sometimes, as with certain Senufo masks, those of the hyena or the baboon, for example, they spit fire from tinder which is burned in the mouth of the animal represented by the mask. When the masks do not appear, they are absent, away in the bush, or, as Dogon children believe, in an anthill of giant ants.

Of course it is only children—and we are not sure of this—who do not know that the masks are worn by men. However, the masks are more than masked men. Among the Dogon, reports Marcel Griaule, the mask is the bearer of *nyama*, "a potential energy, impersonal, unconscious, existing in all human beings, animals, plants, supernatural beings and things, in nature, and it tends to continue its existence in the object to which it is applied." The mask which has absorbed the *nyama* of a dead man becomes potentially very dangerous, and may be handled only by initiated men, members of the *awa*, a mask society. In general, one might say that the wearer or carrier and also the wood or fiber objects he carries lend their physical being to the supernatural being which takes possession of them during rituals or dances. At this time it is the spirit which becomes visible, moves and speaks; it is no longer this man or this carved image, it is a mask.

The men entitled to wear mask usually form societies which anthropologists call secret because only the members know each other to be members, and because they never appear in public as members with their faces uncovered. However, the activities of these societies concern not only their members but the whole group, that is, the village. The societies fulfill religious functions by practising a cult in honor of certain spirits in the name of the whole community, watching to see that certain works of public utility, such as the cleaning of sacred places, are performed at the right time, and to put pressure on those unwilling to conform to certain social rules—refrain from adultery, pay debts, etc. In this respect, the secret society acts as the voice of public opinion or as an agent of coercion in cases where noncoercive social sanctions are not enough. This poses a problem concerning the relationship between political power—the chief—and the secret society: they could enter into competition in a struggle for effective power over the group. In actual fact, it seems that the chief and the masks represent the same social forces or the same special interests, for they seem in general never to oppose each other.

There are other masks which are associated with more pleasant activities. Such are the elegant headpieces in the form of antelopes which are worn on the heads of Bambara dancers and symbolize the semi-human being who taught agriculture. They are worn, writes Germaine Dieterlen, by young men who dance in public in the fields to encourage the workers hoeing millet. Here the mask is the "witness and physical vehicle of the spiritual forces associated with rain and germination." Similarly, among the Yoruba, during the Gelede society ceremonies (a society of men whose function is to celebrate fertility) the masks come out not only at night for the rites but also in the afternoon, to entertain the people. According to Claude Tardits, who remarks on this fact, the masks thus bring religious ceremony into everyday life, "as if mediation between the supernatural and human beings should be accomplished partly through entertainment."

Masks and Myths

With people who, like the Dogon, have a body of knowledge, partly esoteric and highly elaborate, about the origins of the world and of man, masks play a part in their mythical vision: they suggest certain elements of myth, or are embodied in it. The *kanaga* Dogan mask is surmounted by a sort of Cross of Lorraine, to the ends of the arms of which are attached four short boards set parallel to the vertical axis. This form symbolizes man, who in himself suggests creation; the two small animal or human figures at the top of the cross represent the primordial couple who came out of the egg of the world, which contains in seed form the whole of the cosmos.

The Cross of Lorraine itself grows out of simpler forms, one of which represents the creator god, the sky and the earth, another the spiral movement of a god starting into movement. This interpreation is not an ethnographer's inference, but the explanation given to him by those who were initiated into the highest degrees of the cosmological science of the Dogon. Another mask, the *sirige*, which may be more than fifteen feet high, represents a two-story house with eighty niches, suggesting the eighty first ancestors; the dancer traces with this mask a movement from east to west, to imitate the course of the sun.

The Dogon Great Mask is not worn by a dancer: the hollow is not big enough for a man to put his head into, and besides it is about thirty feet tall. Carved out of a large tree, it represents a snake. At one time, when death did not yet exist, men turned into snakes when they grew old. One old man had just undergone this transformation when he met some young men who, in spite of his prohibition, had seized some masks. Very angry, he upbraided them in the language of men, which is forbidden to those who have already taken on the form of an animal of the world of spirits. Having thus become impure for the spirits, he could no longer live with them nor return to the world of men: he died. So that his soul and his energy could have a physical body, a mask was carved in the form of a snake, and sacrifices were made to it, and dances were organized which became a new ceremony, the *sigui*. Since then the Great Mask is ritually exhibited and the *sigui* ceremonies are repeated every sixty years.

Dogon cosmology is symbolized by their masks, as also by their architecture, the plan of their dwellings, the lay-out of their fields, but it is made explicit only in a tradition which is known in its entirety only by a very few Dogon. The idea expressed by this Niger peasant tradition is complex, subtle and abstract. Here is a sketch of it, taken from Griaule and Dieterlen's account. The Dogon conception of the universe is founded on the one hand on a principle of vibrations of matter, and on the other on a general movement of the universe as a whole. The original germ of life is symbolized by the smallest seed of a cultivated plant, that of fonio. This seed, animated by an internal vibration, bursts its skin and comes out to reach as far as the bounds of the universe. At the same time, this developing matter moves in a spiral or helical path. Thus two basic ideas are expressed. On the one hand, the perpetual spiral movement signifies the conservation of matter; in addition, this motion, which is represented graphically by a zig-zag line on the walls of sacred places, is said to symbolize the perpetual alternation of opposites—right and left, high and low, odd and even, male and female—and to reflect a principle of twinship which, ideally, should rule the reproduction of life. These paired opposites maintain a balance which the individual keeps within himself. And also, the infinite extension of the universe is expressed by the continual motion of matter in a spiral path.

Here I see the convergence of two discoveries. Seeking to discern the foundations of African sculpture, Fagg is struck by the frequent appearance in African works of spirals which extend at a constant angle. They "correspond approximately to what mathematicians call exponential or logarithmic curves. In non-mathematical terms, we can recognize these curves in those described by the tusks of elephants and boars and developing horns of the antelope or the ram." Among the examples shown by Fagg—works coming from about ten different societies— there are no Dogon sculptures. He adds that this form, which so obviously expresses a law of growth, is used by the sculptor for its intrinsic beauty and for its affinities with the idea of energy. The dynamic philosophy of the Dogon must be compared with the Luba conception of the world which we summarized previously, its basic premise being that being is vital force. Thus the Dogon peasants explicitly and the Luba cultivators implicitly translate in very similar manner their experience of the reality that surrounds them, affirming that final existence and ultimate value consist of fertile energy, the strength of growth. Thus the Bambara, Senufo, Baga, Yoruba, Ibibio, Huana, Kwele, Luba, Songe and Kuba sculptors have unconsciously chosen the spiral form which the Dogon sages consciously used to symbolize the continual expansion of the universe.

This convergence of similar forms, expressing the same understanding of reality as expanding energy, reminds us that the peasant class of Sudan civilization shares with other African cultivators a basic common experience: that of the man who sows or plants in order to reap. Now cultivators form an important majority in all African civilizations, including the industrial civilization with which we shall deal in the next chapter. The only exception is the civilization of the bow, but for a long time those who live only by hunting and gathering have been a small and diminishing number. We must never lose sight of this important agricultural component which is common to all of Black Africa, for it explains the cultural resemblances which appear across the whole continent south of the Sahara. It is on this basis that develops the special quality of each of the great African civilizations.

Ghana, Land of Gold

The original civilization which developed between the equatorial forest and the Sahara was possible only because of the existence of certain natural resources and the techniques necessary to uitlize them and transport the products.

The most valuable of these resources is gold. The earliest mention of the ancient kingdom of Ghana, in an Arab text from the eleventh century, calls it the land of gold. Raymond Mauny does not hesitate to state that the Sudan was one of the principal suppliers of gold for the Mediterranean world until the discovery of America. The gold came especially from the regions of the sources of the River Senegal.

According to another Arab text, edited by El Bekri in 1067, all the gold nuggets found in the mines of Ghana belonged to the king; the dust was left to the panners. But for these precautions, adds the chronicler, there would be so much gold on the market that its value would decrease. For above all gold was an exchange medium which enabled one to acquire salt, cloth, copper, dates and figs, all products from the north. The caravans organized by Maghreb traders crossed the Sahara by half a dozen trails. Besides gold, they brought to the Mediterranean ivory, ebony, ostrich feathers and slaves.

This concentration and circulation of commodities offered many sources of income to the rulers of Ghana. A commercial tax was imposed on merchandise. El Bekri gives us the tax rate on exported gold and imported salt and copper. The *ghana*—the name is also used as the title of the king—had considerable power: he was able to support a large army and bring in skillful craftsmen to make efficient weapons. Thus the production of gold and other goods gave rise to a large trade circulation. By appropriating part of the profit of this trade the king and a group of rulers were able to develop a state structure and to dominate a vast region extending from the Senegal to the Niger.

When El Bekri published his description, in the middle of the eleventh century, Ghana had already been in existence for several centuries. The kings belonged to the Sarakole group, which still exists and comprises almost 360,000 individuals. Of course their wealth attracted the attention and aroused the envy of their distant neighbors in the Maghreb. Thus, in order to spread Islam, the Almoravids undertook the conquest of the Sudan region. In 1055 they seized the town of Audaghost, which was paying tribute to Ghana and was situated about fifteen days' journey to the north of the capital; they did not succeed in taking Kumbi, the capital, until 1076. This defeat of Ghana had as its consequence conversion to Islam, though perhaps rather a superficial conversion, of part of the population, the ruling group. The absence of all representational art in the towns of the Sudan, contrasting with its abundance in the cities of the Gulf of Benin, is probably due to the Islamization of the Sudanese rulers.

Almoravid domination did not last long, and the prosperity of Ghana continued under the new Black Islamic kings. Several excavations, of which the earliest date from 1914, and the more recent, led by P. Thomassey and R. Mauny, from 1951, allow us to identify almost certainly the site of the capital of Ghana, Kumbi. It is the place now called Kumbi Saleh, about 220 miles north of Bamako, the present capital of Mali. The ruins indicate that the capital was very large, and had about 30,000 inhabitants in the twelfth century, a population which is comparable to that of the medieval cities of Europe, which were also founded on commerce and crafts. (The population of Paris in 1220 has been estimated as about 120,000.) At one end was the royal residence, and at the other, about seven miles away, the quarter of the Muslim traders who had come to establish themselves for business in the capital. According to Mauny's description, "the city itself is built entirely of stone, a gray slate which is found there and which is easily cut into slabs. This is the material used everywhere, for walls, pavements, decorations, stele in the cemeteries, etc. The houses were of more than one story, and the collapse of the upper stories covered the ground floors, which are thus magnificently preserved under about twelve feet of rubble. The center of the city is arranged around a large square, from which several streets lead out. . . . Flagstones on the ground, plaques painted with inscriptions from the Koran on the walls, graceful niches hollowed out of the walls and pillars, stone staircases, not counting a large quantity of high quality materials (iron tools and weapons, pottery, pearls, stone mills and the finest "deneraux" or glass weights for weighing gold) give us a good idea of the civilization which flourished here."

Kumbi was destroyed in 1240. The Susu, who were then reigning in Ghana, were overthrown by Sundiata, the Malinke king of the neighboring empire, Mali, which was to succeed Ghana as the preponderant power of the Western Sudan. The revered name of Ghana, the first Black empire we can still trace, has been taken over by the government of the state which in 1957 succeeded the British colony of the Gold Coast. By this it wanted to indicate not a historic connection—ancient Ghana never extended its domination to the area which is now part of present-day Ghana—but the continuity of an idea, that of an African political sovereignty.

Mali and Songhai

On the other hand, the lands of present-day Mali partly coincide with those of ancient Mali. At its peak, in the fourteenth century, it extended from the Sahara to the forest and from the Atlantic Ocean to Gao. The capital, called Mali, along with the cities of Timbuktu and Djenne were famous centers not only of trade but also of intellectual life. Leo Africanus who lived at Timbuktu at the beginning of the sixteenth century, was struck by the number of judges, doctors and clerks who received high salaries from the king and were regarded with great respect. He noted that books were imported from the Maghreb, and that the profit from them was greater than on any other kind of trade.

A document found in the nineteenth century at Tlemcen, quoted by Henri Labouret, gives a very concrete view of the importance and the organization of trans-Saharan trade between the Mediterranean and Mali at this time. There was a family which originated in the Maghreb, the Makkari. Two brothers had established themselves at Tlemcen where they collected merchandise from Europe and North Africa. Another brother had settled at Sidjilmessa, a caravan terminal: he sent southward the goods which came from Tlemcen, and towards the coast that came from the Sahara. At the other end of the route, at Walata, a Mali city, two younger brothers, who had married local women, received the caravans from the north and warehoused the goods that were sent to them by their partners from various Sudanese cities: skins, cola nuts, ivory, gold dust and slaves. Besides this, due to their agreements with the chiefs of the

Saharan nomads, the Makkari obtained safe-conducts and guides for merchants who wanted to cross the Sahara; they dug and maintained wells along the route.

The most powerful king of Mali, Kankan Musa, reigned from 1307 to 1332. On a pilgrimage to Mecca, he dazzled Cairo with his opulence; it is said that after his departure the value of gold diminished in that city. Under his successors, in the fifteenth century, Mali became weaker: the Tuareg in the north, the Mossi in the south-east, the Songhai in the east threatened and even seized parts of Kankan Musa's empire.

Then the kingdom of Songhai, a former vassal of Mali, took first place in the Sudan region. In the ninth century, the Songhai, coming from Dendi in the north of present-day Dahomey, moved up the Niger and captured Gao, which they made their capital at the beginning of the eleventh century. The kings were converted to Islam and Gao became from that time an important commercial and intellectual city. In 1939 tomb inscriptions were found at Gao, dating from this period. Conquered by Mali under Kankan Musa, Gao soon freed itself, and in the fifteenth century Sonni Ali made Songhai the most powerful state in the Sudan, conquering Timbuktu and Djenne. Although he was a Muslim, he had the reputation of having persecuted the Muslims of Timbuktu and shown a deep understanding of the traditional religions of the Songhai. One of Sonni Ali's lieutenants, Muhammed Ture, overthrew Sonni Ali's son and successor, and founded the new dynasty of the Askia. He added to the Songhai empire and organized its administration: he created a hierarchy of officials, divided the country into districts, appointed a representative of the central power in each city, and established a standing army. During his pilgrimage to Mecca he obtained the title of caliph of the Sudan; he brought many scholars and men of letters into the cities of the Songhai empire, which became such brilliant centers that students came from the Maghreb to take lessons from Black masters. At the end of the sixteenth century an army of Spanish mercenaries was sent by the sultan

of Morocco to capture Gao; because of their arquebuses—the
Africans had no firearms—this undertaking was successful. Having brought back their loot—according to an English witness
quoted by Basil Davidson: thirty camels laden with gold nuggets,
pepper, unicorn horns, eunuchs, dwarfs and slaves and fifteen
virgins, daughters of the king of Gao—the Moroccans and their
mercenaries admitted that they could not keep up the network
of trade relations which brought gold into the markets of the
Sudan, and their domination quickly declined. But they ruined
the cities of the Niger: Timbuktu, Djenne and Gao are now only
stagnant cities. This very brief glimpse of the history of the three
best-known kingdoms of the Sudan—Ghana, Mali and Songhai
—indicates the special nature of the civilization of cities. We
have already encountered kingdoms in the savannas south of the
great equatorial forests and in the high plateaus of eastern and
southern Africa. In these cases, the formation of large political
units was based on agricultural surplus or cattle used as capital;
in the northern kingdoms, the power of the states rests on wealth
produced by the utilization of natural resources and their sale
outside the society. From this fundamental difference, others
result. First, the considerable wealth in money of which these
governments could be assured offered much wider potentials:
they could bring in foreign specialists, scholars or craftsmen,
they could erect important public buildings, they could maintain
a well-equipped professional army, they could import raw materials which were lacking in their own country, such as copper.
Next, these varied activities necessarily created an urban setting:
the many people associated with power had to be gathered
together close to the king: this is the administrative city; all
those who participate in activities involving economic exchange
have to concentrate where merchandise is stored, transformed,
bought and sold: this is the commercial city. Since authority controls and taxes transactions, the two cities are very close or coincide. Besides this, relations between the rulers and the cities on
the one hand, and the peasant masses on the other, are not as

close as in the other civilizations. Of course the city-dwellers' food is produced by the hinterland, and the villagers pay taxes to representatives of the central authorities, but these payments are not the only source of the state's revenue, and certainly not the most important source. Also, the cultural and linguistic diversity of the Sudanese states is much greater than in the other kingdoms. Even when the dynasties of the cities have arisen from the peasant people of the area—the kings of Gao were Songhai—they are distinguished from them by their Muslim religion and their constant relationship with the many foreigners who pass through the cities or take up permanent residence there. Finally, the currents of international trade bring more than mere merchandise: the caravans also bring ideas. The propagation of Islam in the urban centers of the Sudan bears witness to this.

These characteristics of Sudanese societies take account of their dual nature. They are made up of two strata with divergent outlooks. On the lower level, the peasants live by agriculture and herding in a very limited economic sphere, and in political organizations on the village level. They are scarcely affected by Islam, and their social horizon is limited to a homogeneous group, in both language and culture. On the higher level, the city-states, oriented to the outside, are the terminals and the crossroads of a communications network linking them with each other and with the Maghreb. Each of these levels is more or less economically independent of the other. In certain places this independence is so great that one would be justified in placing peasants and city-dwellers in two categories rather than one. We think, for example, of the Massa of Chad, of the Fali in north Cameroon, of the Lobi and Bobo in the north of the Ivory Coast, of the Koniagi and the Basari of Guinea, who are among the most self-contained groups. These are extreme cases; in areas near cities, rivers and trails, the activities of peasants and city-dwellers are more integrated under the preponderant influence of the town.

Because the peasants of the Sudan have much in common with the other Black farmers, and because Islam comes from outside Africa, we are tempted to find the peasant class more "African" than the city-dwelling class. This is due to a cultural purism (which is as illusory as racial purism), according to which only the oldest forms of a culture are "authentic" because they arose in their own society and were not borrowed from another. In any culture, the origin of a trait matters little; it is its integration in the social heritage of a group that makes it an authentic element of its culture. The Islam of the Sudanese cities is as African as the Christianity of Charlemagne is European.

Sao, Hausa, Fulani

Though the cities of the kingdoms of Ghana, Mali and Songhai are the best known to us, many other cities arose between the Atlantic, the Nile and the Bight of Benin. The ruins of Sao cities, revealed by the excavations of Annie and Jean-Paul Lebeuf, suggest a mysterious civilization which developed about the beginning of the tenth century, probably to the south-east of Lake Chad. According to the traditions of the present inhabitants of the region, the Kotoko, the Sao seem to have been giants of prodigious strength. They are credited with the building of all the walled cities on semi-artificial mounds. At Goulfeil the city wall is still kept in repair. It is trapezoidal in section and about thirty feet high. Jean-Paul Lebeuf notes that "the massiveness of these constructions is amazing in a land without stone, where all available wood is reserved for the reinforcement of roofs and doors." The other Kotoko cities "are far different from what they were in their early days, and all we now see is, with rare exceptions, towns of tumbledown houses clustered at one end of the mound, pictures of disintegrating communities." According to the list of dynasties collected by Lebeuf, the seventy-fifth king of Goulfeil was enthroned in 1947; the first twenty-three kings were Sao and the later ones Muslims.

A Sao is said to have built the city wall of Kano, as the Muslims did not know this technique. Kano is one of the seven Hausa cities which are situated between the River Niger and Lake Chad. According to the legend they were founded by a descendant of the Queen of Daura and his six sons. The history of Kano goes back to the eleventh century. Here we find the usual events: conversion of the kings to Islam (in the fourteenth century), wars against other Hausa cities, especially Zaria, Katsena (fifteenth century), Songhai invasion (sixteenth century). Around the cities the Hausa practised agriculture, and in their fortified towns craftsmanship played an important economic role. Iron, copper and wool were worked. Weaving and dyeing techniques produced fine clothes that were much sought after. These products of craftsmanship were exported to the other cities of the Sudan and the Maghreb. Visiting Kano in the middle of the nineteenth century, Heinrich Barth estimated the quantity of cloth dyed annually at Timbuktu alone as three hundred camel loads, and he estimated that the total return from the exportation of cloth was enough to support from 5000 to 6000 families. Kano also sold abroad about 5000 slaves a year. And the Kano that Barth knew had been in decline for a century, especially since the conquest of the Hausa cities at the beginning of the nineteenth century.

The Fulani have a special place among the peoples of the savanna. They are at present scattered from Futa Toro, in Senegal and Futa Jallon, in Guinea, to Adamawa in Cameroon. Their physical features, rather different from those of other Africans of the area, have given rise to some very fanciful hypotheses about their origin: they have been said to be, on hardly any evidence, descendants of Gypsies, Israelites, Indians, Persians, etc. Whatever their origin, at the beginning of the eleventh century groups of Fulani pastoralists led a wandering life in Futa Toro; in the fifteenth century, some Fulani settled at Macina, north of the Niger; in the sixteenth and seventeenth centuries they formed a state in Futa Jallon. During the eighteenth century the Fulani of Futa Toro settled in the kingdom of Gober, one of the seven Hausa city-states; at the beginning of the nineteenth century one of the Fulani chiefs, Usman dan Fodio, a man of science and of faith, preached a holy war against the Hausa of Gober and seized their kingdom, then Kano, Zaria and Katsena. That was the end of the Hausa city-states.

In the chapter devoted to the civilization of the spear, analysis of the situation of pastoralism in East Africa led us to the conclusion that warrior-herdsmen in contact with farming societies either raid them, if they are passing through, or dominate them, forming a caste society, if they are settling permanently in farming country. The sedentary peoples who encountered the Fulani were not merely village cultivators; behind the cultivators was often the power of rulers of cities who would not allow their peasants to be conquered. When they settled permanently in an area, the Fulani, specialists in cattle-raising, modestly became the herdsmen of the cultivators' cattle. It became the custom to entrust all the animals to the Fulani, who thus came into effective possession of considerable wealth. To profit by this situation and reverse their subordinate position, the Fulani had to be very much aware of their identity and of their opposition to the peasants. They had to unite their small scattered groups and their ideology had to press for this revolutionary action. Islam provided all this, and the Fulani, some groups of whom had remained pagan until the eighteenth century, converted to Islam, seized the cattle, retained them, and subjugated the farmers.

From Lake Chad to the Nile, other cities and other kingdoms arose, flourished, and, very often, disappeared during the last thousand years: Kanem, whose history begins for us in the eleventh century; Bornu, whose high point came at the end of the sixteenth century: Wadai, formed as a state before the fourteenth century but converted to Islam only in the seventeenth; Baguirmi, which became a kingdom in the sixteenth century; Darfur, where the ruins of the town of Jebel Uri remind A. J. Arkell of certain Mero monuments: and Kordofan, which

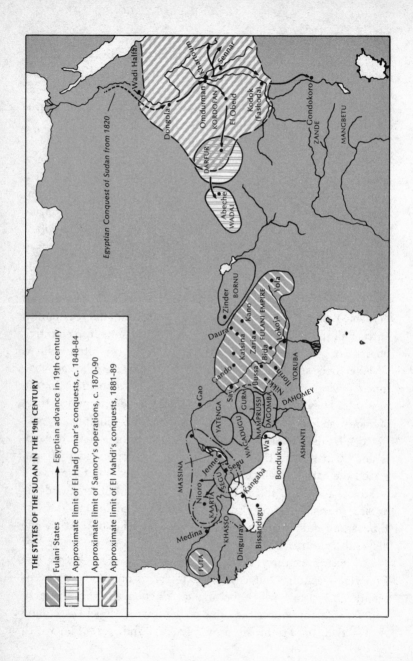

THE STATES OF THE SUDAN IN THE 19TH CENTURY

Fulani States

→ Egyptian advance in 19th century

Approximate limit of El Hadj Omar's conquests, c. 1848–84

Approximate limit of Samory's operations, c. 1870–90

Approximate limit of El Mahdi's conquests, 1881–89

Egyptian Conquest of Sudan from 1820

Wadi Halfa

Dongola

Khartoum

Omdurman

KORDOFAN

El Obeid

Sennar

Kodok (Fashoda)

DARFUR

Abeche

WADAI

Gondokoro

ZANDE

MANGBETU

Zinder

BORNU

Yola

Daura

Katsina

Kano

Zaria

FULANI EMPIRE

Kokoja

Gando

Bida

Bussa

Ilorin

YORUBA

Gao

NIKKI

DAHOMEY

Say

YATENGA

GURMA

MOSSI

WAGADUGU

MAMPRUSSI

DAGOMBA

Wa

ASHANTI

MASSINA

Jenne

Nioro

KAARTA

Sego

SEGU

Kangaba

Bonduku

Medina

KHASSO

Dinguiray

Bissandugu

FUTA

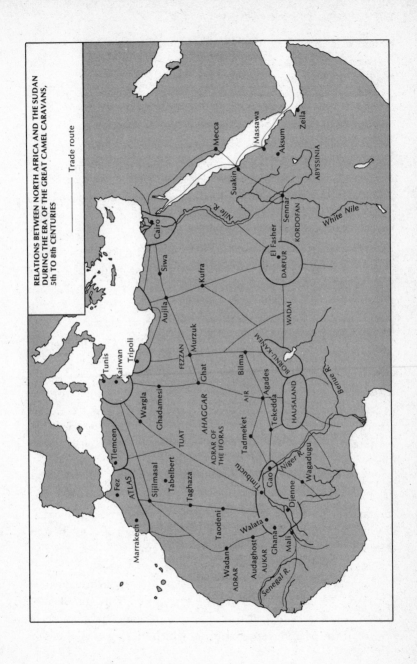

RELATIONS BETWEEN NORTH AFRICA AND THE SUDAN DURING THE ERA OF THE GREAT CAMEL CARAVANS, 5th TO 8th CENTURIES

——— Trade route

extended to the White Nile. From the cities in the eastern part of the Sudan savanna, caravan trails led not only directly to the Mediterranean, but also to the Nile.

The Cities of the South

The civilization of cities is not restricted to the edges of the Sahara—dry steppes and savanna. To the south of this zone, other societies show a similar structure; they are urban, commercial, manufacturing, outward-looking. But there are important differences: Islam is not the religion of the rulers of the city-states; relations with the outside world are by sea and with the countries of Western Europe; the natural habitat is savanna with varied vegetation, but clearly a richer vegetation than that of the north: we are approaching the sea and the great Atlantic forest, home of the civilization of the clearings.

As in the steppes, the formation of political units is not due to foreign influences; when the first European navigators arrived, at the end of the fifteenth or the beginning of the sixteenth century, the Yoruba and Bini cities were already in existence; the kingdoms of Kumasi and Abomey, which were formed in the seventeenth and eighteenth centuries, arose and developed according to a process that is familiar to us and which owes nothing to the West: the states farthest from the coast, such as the Nupe, "Black Byzantium," were not visited by Europeans until the beginning of the nineteenth century. The presence of the Europeans on the Atlantic coast was superficial and purely commercial before the colonial period, of which we shall speak in the next chapter. Portuguese, French, English, Dutch and Danes came in search of gold, ivory, pepper, and especially, slaves.

The export of slaves, sending them to the New World plantations—and also, as is not so well known, to Portugal itself—hardly deserves to be called trade. It is not comparable in scale to that of the Mediterranean traffic, which, during the whole of the Middle Ages, supplied slaves from Africa and Europe to the Muslim countries. Unfortunately the figures are very fragmentary. Robin Hallett estimates that at least fifteen million Africans were forcibly transported across the Atlantic during the period of the slave trade, the numbers increasing steadily throughout that period, reaching a maximum of 100,000 a year in the first decades of the nineteenth century. In addition, an equal number probably died during the Atlantic crossings. Such a drain on the population could have only the most serious consequences for societies whose population was at that time neither large nor closely settled. Such impoverishment could not be balanced by an equivalent economic gain. In fact, the slave trade ruined the cultures of the African groups, which, especially on the coast, procured slaves for the European slave traders: wars increased in number and destructiveness; they were fought for the purpose of taking captives, and to defend one's freedom and often one's life; the distance between rulers and their commoner subjects, who might at some time be sold, increased and became unbridgeable; respect for life diminished and executions and cruel sacrifices increased. Daryll Forde has edited the diary of Antera Duke, an Efik chief who trafficked in slaves in the eighteenth century at Calabar (on the coast of present-day Nigeria). This diary presents, in its brief and factual daily entries, a vivid picture of this social disintegration.

In spite of the slave trade, the civilization of cities experienced brilliant successes in the south. An example is the cities of the Yoruba country. The Yoruba, who now number more than four million, and in the nineteenth century lived in large cities (Ibadan, 200,000 inhabitants; Ogbomosho and Iwo, 60,000 each; Oshogbo, 40,0000; and about ten cities of more than 20,000 inhabitants), had elaborated a complex political organization. Through recognizing the supreme authority in religious matters of the *oni* of Ife, and in political matters of the *alafin* of Oyo, each city administered itself. Municipal power was vested in two institutions: the *ogboni*, a cultural and political association of notables, and the *bale,* a chief appointed by the *ogboni* for a limited term of office, with officials to assist them.

The economic foundation of Yoruba society is unusually secure because of its diversity. The Yoruba cultivate yams, cola, bananas, palm nuts, maize, manioc and peanuts (the three last introduced from America as a consequence of the slave trade); they raise cattle; hunting and fishing are supplementary activities. They mine iron and make hoes, axes and adzes; they also work gold, silver, bronze and brass. The women, using a vertical loom and the men, using a horizontal loom, weave cloth which is then dyed. They carve wood and make pottery. Trade between regions is important. Not only valuables but also ordinary manufactured objects and even agricultural products are exchanged among Yoruba towns.

Thus, before the industrial period, Africa experienced an urban civilization based on manufacture and trade, which is fundamentally analogous to the civilization of the commercial cities of the European Middle Ages. This social and cultural phenomenon is not limited to a few exceptional cases; it has been exemplified for centuries in many societies spread over a vast area of the African continent. Our picture of this civilization is far from complete. Discoveries by archaeologists and historians have greatly enriched it in less than twenty years. There are still cultures like Kumbi Saleh, Jebel Uri, Nok, Sao, perhaps Benin, to dig out of the steppes, the savanna and the palm groves.

Contemporary folk sculpture, Uganda

Pottery, Kisalian culture (7th-8th century, A.D.), Sanga, Congo-Kinshasa

Contemporary "academic" sculpture, Kampala, Uganda

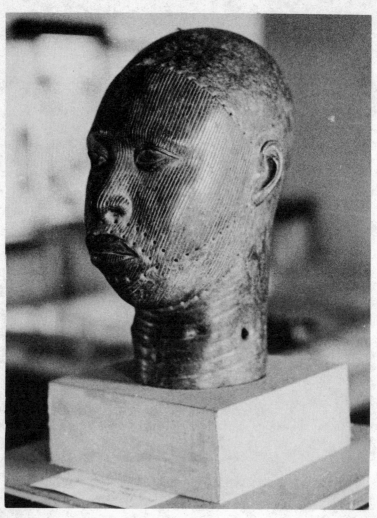

Ife head. Ife Museum, Nigeria

King's stool, Ashanti, Ghana

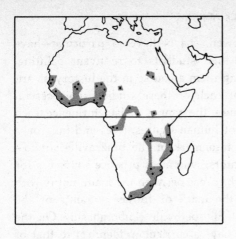

THE CIVILIZATION
OF INDUSTRY

Visual Arts and Dance Music

In the art schools of Dakar, Accra, Ibadan, Brazzaville, Kinshasa, Kampala and Lubumbashi, in the innumerable art studios scattered in the towns of Black Africa, in the thousands of bars where dance music is played, the art forms of contemporary Africa are coming to birth. Here we find little trace of the powerful serenity of traditional sculpture, the majestic breadth of village dances, the refined opulence of the court arts. Yet this is an exciting art, varied, lively, and, despite influences and borrowings, original.

Several artists in African art schools—Pierre-Romain Desfossés,

André Lodts, Frank McEwen, Iba N'diaye in particular—have done their best to allow their students to re-invent painting, even refraining from giving them a course in the history of art. However, the products of each of these studios show certain similarities, perhaps because the young artists influence each other. Hence, silhouettes of human figures, trees and huts on a dark background are the trademark of the Brazzaville studio—and also of its many imitators, who mass produce souvenirs for tourists; hence, filling in the areas between the main motifs with colored lines or dots is the mark of former students of the Institut des Beaux-Arts of Elisabethville (Lubumbashi). On the other hand, other schools have a curriculum identical to that of European schools and produce good craftsmen.

Certain techniques of traditional art have fallen into disuse: why forge iron or make pottery when you can find imported knives of better quality, and aluminum containers which are cheaper and stronger? Others such as wood sculpture have remained unchanged, but rarely in the same context as in the old days. The statues may look like the ritual ancestor figures, but they are no longer used ceremonially; they are secular objects, and are used only to decorate the home of somebody who is usually a stranger to the sculptor's society. And since lovers of the picturesque are seldom gifted with sound aesthetic taste, the craftsman does not set himself a very high standard: his customers are looking for a cheap knick-knack rather than a work of quality. However, when an artist has the advantage of an educated and demanding public, he can create fine pieces in the tradition of his culture.

The popular music of urban centers—the high-life of the West Coast cities, for example—betrays a very strong influence from Latin American dance music and jazz; the guitar has become the most important instrument. However, this music is not slavishly copied, it is reinterpreted; in the same way, the style of dancing in couples is different from what it was until recently in the United States and Europe: though in perfect harmony, the bodies of the partners do not touch. This music and these dances are perhaps the most living part of urban culture; the small groups are constantly renewing their repertoire and enliven the bars, which are the focus of a strong community life in the cities. After a day's work, the bar offers workers the relaxation which they cannot find in their small overcrowded homes. They let the rhythm take hold of them and, silently dancing, escape into dream. They drink, and buy drinks for unattached women. These women are not prostitutes, but the temporary partners of solitary men who have left their villages and their families to work for a time in the city; the women cook and keep house for them. They bring to the bar the gaiety of clothes in bright, tastefully combined colors, the grace of their swaying walk, the dazzle of their laughter.

This state of the arts in the most recent of the great African civilizations has aroused nostalgia and denunciation. People recall the brilliant artistic traditions that developed in the other African civilizations and reproach the artists for allowing themselves to be influenced by foreign trends and for losing the purity and originality of the traditional works. It is true, but it could not be otherwise. The artistic standards of what we call the civilization of industry betrays two characteristics of this civilization: its full participation in world-wide trends, and its attempts to find a new balance. The preponderance of jazz and Latin American rhythms in popular music is not a phenomenon peculiar to Africa, it is common to all the cities of the industrial areas of Europe, American, Australia and some Asian countries, such as Japan. One could even argue that Africa has more reasons than Europe to adopt this popular music, since its own traditional music, brought over by slaves into the New World, was one of the sources of Latin American dance music, and jazz. But the question of origin is secondary; because of records, radio, the cinema, weekly illustrated magazines, popular culture has become unified, and spreads everywhere where mass communications exist, and it happens that, for the time being, the musical part of this universal culture is based on jazz and Latin American dance music. Their success in Africa indicates that the masses of the industrial centers participate in the same popular culture as most of the other working people of the world. Thus, on the level of leisure and escape, the peoples of Africa show how they have taken their place in major world trends.

The visual arts express even more the ambiguities of the new civilization, divided between the traditional values which people cannot bring themselves to forsake, and the promises of the modern world. Especially to the Black intellectuals, aware of their Africanity, this problem appears in the form of a painful choice. They refuse the extreme positions, either total rejection of the West and its techniques or complete adoption of the totality of European civilization, but inquire into the possibility of a new synthesis.

Westernization or Industrialization

Let us first note that although it is convenient to contrast "the West" and "traditional Africa," these terms do not appropriately express, they even mask, the true contrasts. Actually, the new civilization which has arisen in Africa differs from the other African civilizations in that it is founded on industry; which is the source of its specific nature. Now, although the revolution resulting from this new technique or production occurred historically first in Great Britain, then in some other European countries, it cannot, now, in the middle of the twentieth century, be identified with "the West." Do we think that to introduce the manufacture of paper into a country constitutes Sinification? And yet paper is a Chinese invention dating from the first century A.D., which did not reach Europe until the twelfth century, through a series of well-known stages. To be industrialized does not mean to be Westernized, it only means, to adopt certain production techniques which first developed in Europe but which quickly became common to a large number of societies, which improved them in many ways. It is therefore more correct to pose the problem in the following terms: can social structures, world views, and works of art which arose in nonindustrial civilizations persist in industrial societies?

Not until the end of this chapter, after we have deciphered some of the directions written into the earliest developments of the industrial civilization of contemporary Africa will we try to give a few basic answers to this question.

The six civilizations we have described still exist in contemporary Africa. Hunters still range the forests, steppes and savannas; they also use francs and shillings to buy shirts and soap. Cultivators still grow root crops in the forest clearings and grain in the savannas, and their children learn to read in rural schools. Hereditary chiefs keep the drums that symbolize their authority; but they must account for their administration to the Ministry of the Interior. Herdsmen tend their great herds; they also make butter and cheese in cooperative dairies. Cotton is woven, leather is cut, wood is worked, but in textile factories, shoe factories and carpenters' shops. . . . Thus all the great traditional occupations are carried on, yet all are somewhat modified.

Over and above this, activities which did not exist in any of the civilizations have become the chief occupations of millions of Africans: mining, accountancy, the teaching of mathematics, assembling tractors, driving trains, performing surgical operations, directing transport enterprises, measuring drug dosages, repairing engines. . . .

These new activities and modifications of traditional ones do not form a blend of disparate elements, but are organized into a totality which is a unity, though an imperfect one. People who live in societies in which this pattern of activities is predominant, have built around it an appropriate and distinctive way of life, a culture. These societies are scattered over all the regions of Black Africa, especially in the new settlements which have arisen and rapidly grown around industrial enterprises, ports and commercial junctions and administrative centers. The cultures of these different groups display such strong similarities that they may be considered as part of the same civilization.

This civilization has been called modern, literate, bureaucratic, technological, commercial, monetary. It is, of course, all these, but I think that its basic quality is that of being industrial; a quality symbolized by steel, the essential material of industrial machinery. Industry is a technique of producing material goods which uses large sources of energy and expensive equipment; these characteristics make possible and necessary a high level of production, so that its productivity is higher than that of handicrafts. Industrial technology is unevenly distributed in Black Africa. Highly developed in South Africa and the copper belt of Zambia and northern Katanga, and in some parts of West Africa, it is almost nonexistent in vast areas. Other "modern" phenomena, such as formal education, bureaucratic administration, rapid transport, by road, rail and air, are much more widespread in contemporary Africa. Why, then, give priority to industrial technology?

Because the two great political waves which have submerged Black Africa during the last hundred years—colonization, then independence, both closely linked with industry—have their origin in certain phases of industrialization, first in Europe, then in Africa itself. Because industrial technology is at the heart of the solution to problems crucial to the young African states on the economic level (underdevelopment), on the political level (real independence), and on the philosophic and artistic level (intellectual Africanity). Because the section of the population directly linked with industrial activities, and thus with urban life, has had and will continue to have a leading role in the choices of modern Africa. Because these techniques of production, everywhere they have been introduced, have had consequences which have had such a profound effect on societies and cultures that we may speak of an "industrial revolution"; there is no reason why this "revolution", which is not yet complete

in the countries which were the first to be industrialized, should
not have equally profound and lasting effects in Africa.

The Colonial Period

Enterprises such as Arab settlements in the east coast ports,
European clearing-houses for the trade in ivory, gold and slaves
on the West Coast, Arab way stations on the southern edge of
the Sahara, are not colonial undertakings. Likewise, the installa-
tion of the Portuguese in the fifteenth century in the Kingdom
of the Kongo, and that of the Dutch of the East India Company
in the eighteenth century near the Cape of Good Hope, are more
like forerunners of colonialism. Not until the second half of the
nineteenth century did the European powers divide among themselves the interior of the continent to establish their empires. The
Conference of Berlin in 1885 set the rules for this partition such
as: possession of the coast gives the right to the corresponding
region of the interior; effective occupation of a territory is necessary if the sovereignty of the occupier is to be recognized by the
other powers. This territorial expansion was the act of the industrialized countries of Western Europe, and was the result of
economic necessity.

In Europe, the production of consumer goods was the first
sector to be industrialized: was not Manchester a textile center?
At this time, the process of the system required each undertaking
to increase the volume of its production so that its prices could
still be competitive, and thus to sell more and more. The available European market for consumer goods was not enough,
especially since wages were kept as low as possible during the
first period of industrialization. Thus it was necessary constantly
to seek new markets. It was equally necessary to procure for
these manufacturing industries more and cheaper raw materials,
such as cotton and rubber. Finally, so that the European masses
of workers could attain an acceptable standard of living without

receiving higher wages, it was useful to import various goods very cheaply, especially foodstuffs such as coffee and cocoa. The colonization of Africa enabled new markets to be opened for industrially manufactured goods, and to obtain in payment raw materials for manufacture, and agricultural products for immediate consumption.

When industrial technology was extended to capital goods, they too had to be exported. This is especially true of railways. The abundant mineral wealth discovered in Africa offered vast possibilities to European heavy industry. First, their utilization required mining centers to be equipped, long-distance railways to be constructed, and ports built; then, the mines produced a variety of minerals which, processed in Europe, supplied the raw materials for the steel industry.

Thus Africa itself became industrialized. Around the mines, secondary industries were established. Dwellings, shops, roads were built; and also schools, for workers who could translate, type and handle figures were required. The process of colonization, once under way, went beyond what was necessary for the development of commercial enterprises, vast plantations of crops, for export mining companies, manufacturing industries. This is always the case with broad historical trends. In the case of Black Africa, various secondary forces acted in directions which did not always accord with the general orientation produced by the requirements of the technico-economic situation.

The colonial governments were reluctant to recognize the existence of these requirements, and justified their colonial policies by loftier reasons: to free the Black people from Arab slave-traders, to lead them towards progress, to accomplish a "civilizing mission." These declarations of the explicit aims of colonization made it necessary, under pressure from certain sections of colonial public opinion to take a few steps in accordance with these objectives, such as the recognition of the freedom to form trade unions, organization of education on the university level, regulation of work conditions and fixing minimum wages. On the other hand, groups pursuing their own goals, such as Christian missions, institutes of scientific research, organizations for assistance and education, established themselves in Africa.

Colonization, by spreading knowledge of European languages, established contact, by means of reading, with the political trends of the modern world and its major themes: equality between all men, the right to participate in the government of one's society, the value of the dignity of the individual and of liberty. Bringing workers into a monetary system, colonization introduced them into a world where the things that make life pleasant were all around them. This wonderful wealth was right at hand, possessed and displayed by Europeans living in the colonies, but inaccessible to the African workers, since the amount they could buy with their wages was insignificant.

Political Independence

Thus the colonial system carried within itself the seeds of its own destruction. The Africans, aware of their own strength, worked to achieve their goal of political independence. The results were startling. In ten years, from 1956 to 1966, thirty-one independent states were formed out of colonial territories: The Sudanese Republic (formerly the Anglo-Egyptian Sudan), Ghana —(Gold Coast)— (1957); Guinea (1958); Mauretania, Senegal, Mali (French Sudan), Upper Volta, Ivory Coast, Togo, Dahomey, Niger, Chad, Cameroon, Nigeria, Central African Republic (Ubangi-Shari), Gabon, Congo-Brazzaville (French Congo); Congo-Kinshasa (Belgian Congo) Somalia (Italian and British Somaliland), these sixteen states in 1960; in 1961, Tanganyika and Sierra Leone; in 1962, Uganda, Rwanda, Burundi (the two latter states formed by dividing the Trust Territory of Ruanda-Urundi); in 1963, Kenya and Zanzibar (which in 1964 united with Tanganyika to form Tanzania); in 1964, Malawi (former

Nyasaland) and Zambia (former Northern Rhodesia); in 1965 Gambia; finally, in 1966, Botswana (Bechuanaland) and Lesotho (Basutoland.)

These accessions to independence were achieved remarkably peacefully if one considers the enormous political revolution which made possible the birth of each of these young nations. The most serious disturbances that occurred (those which marked the formation of the Republic of the Congo (Kinshasa, formerly Leopoldville) were not nearly so severe as the bitter and bloody struggles against colonialism of some nations in other parts of the world. These relatively calm and peaceful changes were due on the one hand to the political skill and moderation of most of the African leaders, who preferred gradual evolution to sudden uprootings; on the other hand to the resignation of the colonial governments to the inevitable disengagement. Nowhere did they attempt outright resistance.

This conciliatory attitude was certainly due in part to the conviction that a colonial system is an outmoded political form, an opinion sufficiently widespread in the countries of Western Europe to make a colonial war very unpopular. Also, the economic exigencies which had made the political occupation of Africa necessary in the nineteenth century no longer existed. In the nineteenth century political domination was necessary to enlist Africa, with its consumers, its labor force and its wealth of foodstuffs and minerals, as a subordinate partner in the socioeconomic system of Europe. In the middle of the twentieth century, the economic structures which had organized the subordination of African undertakings into huge systems, directed by colonial financial groups for their own profit, had been firmly established. It now seemed that they could be maintained without any basic change in a context of political independence. Had not some Latin American republics set an example of the possible coexistence of political independence with economic dependence? Besides, some European capitalist circles were going even farther on the way to disengagement. They reckoned that certain basic expenses (communications, equipment of cihes, etc.) and social expenses (hospitals, schools, etc.) were becoming so large that the profits of private investments would no longer be enough to justify the continuation of colonialism. Since the colonies were to cost more than they were to bring in, it was better not to make any effort to retain political domination. This "doctrine" of disengagement known in France as "Cartierisme," after the journalist Raymond Cartier, seems to have played some part in the unexpected decisions by the Belgian government, in January 1960, to bestow in June of the same year "total and immediate independence" on its Congo colony, "a country held until that time in complete colonial dependence, a country which had no native elite, no experience of democracy or administrative techniques." (Hubert Deschamps)

A Settlers' Resistance

The total outcome of these circumstances—the wisdom of African statesmen, division of financial opinion about the prospects for capital investment in underdeveloped countries, the desire of governments to avoid colonial wars—made it relatively easy for many colonial lands of Black Africa to achieve political independence. However, this was not everywhere the case. The principal obstacle was the presence in some colonies of minorities of permanently established European settlers. These minorities have a strong and direct interest in the maintenance of the colonial regime, an interest which is not shared by other groups which also operate within the colonial framework. Administrative officials, European employees of large industrial and commercial enterprises, missionaries, the personnel of teaching and research institutions, enjoyed many advantages from the colonial situation, but still maintained their orientation towards their home countries where they had been recruited, where they spent their leaves, where their families lived, and where they expected to settle permanently at the end of their careers. The settlers, on the other hand, especially the farmers, had settled in Africa because of the advantages offered to them by the colonial regime: the best land could be obtained at a low price, the African farmers could be prevented by various means from competing with their prices. This privileged position made possible a life style which had disappeared in the countries of Western Europe after the French Revolution. Thus the colonists defended forcefully, sometimes even desperately, the colonial system which alone could guarantee their privileges. This is why decolonization met with much greater difficulties where the settlers constituted important minorities, as in Rhodesia (4,800,000 Africans, 250,000 Europeans) where they formed about five per cent of the population.

In South Africa, the European minority is the largest in Africa (3,000,000 Europeans to 12,000,000 Africans) and in certain parts of the country has been deeply rooted for several generations. These settlers have succeeded in doing what their counterparts in other African countries have only dreamed of, what the Rhodesian settlers have achieved only by 1965: cutting themselves off from the mother country, where public opinion no longer allows extreme measures of discrimination or exploitation to be carried out. They have formed a state with hierarchical castes, each with a different status, with respect to the law. This social organization is doing all it can to set up a structure of inequality designed to maintain the privileges of the European minority. For this reason the situation of the European colonists is much stronger in the Republic of South Africa than in the colonial dependencies. However, it is doubtful whether the South African whites will long succeed in maintaining their racist state. For them as for the white minorities in the remaining colonies, the question is no longer one of the possibility of maintaining the status quo, but of their degree of obstinacy in defending it. If they violently resist any change which threatens their privileges, they risk compromising not only those privileges but even the very possibility of continuing to live on African soil.

Another obstacle to peaceful decolonization may arise from the vicissitudes of politics in the home country. The obstinacy of the Portuguese government in pursuing a narrowly conservative policy in Angola and Mozambique seems to be linked with the frailty of a regime at home based in the grandeur of a glorious past. Of course the rulers fear that their government could not withstand the repercussions of the liberation of the Portuguese "provinces" of Africa—a legal fiction which deceives nobody—which would be so incompatible with official ideology.

In the history of African societies, the colonial period will appear as a very brief episode. Its importance lies in having introduced to Africa industrial technology, the basis of a new civilization. This civilization has not yet attained its full growth anywhere, and in some places its presence has hardly yet been felt. But it is already, and certainly will continue to be, the civilization of modern Africa.

Urban Life

The geographical basis of this civilization can be delineated, although unlike other civilizations, it is not a natural region. The areas of densest population on a map of Africa indicate the places where this civilization is most intense and the centers from which it is gradually spreading. Certainly not all African cities have arisen from colonization. We dwelt enough on this when we made the administrative, commercial, manufacturing city the characteristic and the symbol of one of the traditional civilizations. But there are many new settlements and also many traditional cities which have been transformed into cities of the new kind.

Of course the total number of Africans living in cities is not yet very large. According to a seminar of the Economic Commission for Africa held in June 1969, they numbered in 1965 about 48 million for the whole of Africa, which represented 15 per cent of the total population at that time. But urban popula-

tion is increasing very rapidly. Here are a few especially important figures. The population of Dakar increased from 18,400
inhabitants (1904) to 383,000 (1960); Accra from 17,900 (1901)
to 325,900 (1960); Ibadan from 200,000 (1890) to 459,000
(1952), Leopoldville from 4700 (1908) to 389,000 (1958); Luanda
from 11,600 (1860) to 220,000 (1960); Nairobi from 11,500
(1906) to 250,800 (1960); Salisbury from 20,100 (1927) to
192,800 (1958); Bulawayo from 18,600 (1927) to 183,000 (1958).

Even if he lives in a settlement of only a few tens of thousands,
the African workman—or white-collar worker—has an urban
way of life very different from the cultures which developed
among peasants, herdsmen, craftsmen or hunters.

His home is purchased, rented or allotted to him by his em-
ployer; he hardly ever builds it himself with the help of members
of his lineage. If he attempts this on the outskirts of a city
(elsewhere, it is prohibited) it cannot be a traditional hut which
is comfortable to live in, but will be a shantytown hovel. Because
of the rapid growth of the urban population, there is a perpetual
housing crisis, and those who do have a decent dwelling can
house in it only their wives and children. The obligations implied
in the solidarity of the lineage can be fulfilled only in part and at
the cost of great discomfort. How can a maternal uncle, living in
the city, take care of the upbringing of his sister's sons and
daughters when he is anxious to keep his own children with him
so that they can take advantage of the better educational facili-
ties of the city?

The African city-dweller does not grow what is necessary to
his subsistence. He is a wage-earner, and he buys all the goods
he consumes. This kind of income considerably limits his ability
to assist his relatives. If he could manage to house them, he
would still have to feed them for long months, and his wages are
not enough.

Urban life is incompatible with a polygymous family structure.
In the traditional civilizations, the cultivator with several wives
was richer than the man with one, since each wife had fields

which she made productive. But city conditions make the support of more than one wife a serious economic burden.

Village communities were very homogeneous groups. Often a large number of kinsmen lived in the same village. People usually lived in the village where they had been born and grown up. They knew everybody personally. Thus the advice of old men was listened to, and fear of being excluded from the group was sufficient for social control. A city population is heterogeneous and mobile. One lives among strangers whose conduct must be controlled by sanctions backed by force.

The authority of the chiefs of small local communities was based mainly on the principle of heredity. This type of legitimacy does not apply in urban centers: one cannot imagine a mayor handing down his political office to his heir. The holders of local power can only be either named by national authorities, or elected. Even in the colonial period, certain political institutions, termed "noncustomary," had been created because it was so clear that the traditional chiefdoms could not supply a framework for the government of urban centers. Actually, the chiefs were able to run the villages directly because public affairs were rather simple. In an industrial town, administration is so complex that one man could not have the whole responsibility and with it the power of decision, in sectors as varied as primary education, hospital and medical services, road services, distribution of water, traffic police, etc.

The few elements we have mentioned—housing, wages, nuclear family, heterogeneity, local administration—distinguish very sharply this new way of life, which Georges Balandier calls the Black urban culture, from the ways of life characteristic of the other African civilizations. The abandonment of traditional forms —a phenomenon usually called "detribalization"—originates more from urban conditions, which make certain traditional institutions objectively impossible, than from a psychological attitude of rejection of the past. During the first decades of urban life, many compromise solutions were invented by African city-dwellers. At this time the colonial authorities and industrial employers, fearing the creation of a powerful proletariat, tried to limit the process of urbanization, although it was essential for industry. They hoped to reconcile the demands of industry and protect the colonial order by making it very difficult for workers and their families to establish themselves permanently in the cities. Thus in South Africa and Northern and Southern Rhodesia, workers were recruited in their villages, often very far from the mines, and went alone, for the duration of their long contracts, to the center where they were to work. In the Belgian Congo, ownership of a lot in an urban center could not be acquired by a private person. Everywhere else the mere absence of help for a worker trying to establish himself in a town was enough to make things very difficult for him. Thus the temporary city-dwellers kept their ties with their home villages, where their rights to their lands were maintained, and they returned there at the end of their active lives and during periods of unemployment, since there was no unemployment compensation in the city. This situation was very burdensome for the traditional villages; deprived of many men in the prime of life, they still had to keep up a high level of agricultural production to feed all the city-dwellers. Most of the latter also tried to cultivate a small plot of land around their houses or on the outskirts of the city. This preoccupation, together with the policy of building cheap, one-story houses, contributed to the excessive growth in the area of the town, and obliged workers to travel considerable distances between home and work.

The New Nations

The civilization of industry dominates the life of the new towns, but its influence was not limited to this. By way of the colonial administration, it had even reached places very far from towns and roads, at least by that very rudimentary form of contact which consists in the payment of a head tax. The effects of this tax are considerable, for money was needed to pay it, which obliged the most isolated peasants to seek paid employment or to sell some product from their fields to get it. This was the first step towards participation in a money economy.

But for many villagers the influence of the new economy was felt much more strongly. Roads were built between the mines and the ports; it was made compulsory to grow cotton, coffee and peanuts, and this produce was sold to cotton companies or to export bureaus. Farm products for local consumption were sold and consumer goods (clothes, soap, records, beer, etc.) were imported or sometimes manufactured locally. Elementary schools were opened almost everywhere.

Thus during the colonial period an infrastructure was built up within each colony. The boundaries of the colonies had been set very arbitrarily in the nineteenth century, without taking into account political units or traditional cultures. The colonial administrations, never forgetting the maxim "Divide and rule" did not approve of the arousal of feelings of attachment to the colonial political unit.

In addition, the situation of political dependence constituted an obstacle to such feelings, for the Africans clearly saw what the colony really was: a foreign power which organized their lives as a part of social forces and interests which were not their own. The situation changed when, in the last years of the colonies, the right of Africans to participate in public affairs was recognized to some degree, first on the local level and in an advisory capacity, then gradually moving up to a provincial and even central level, with executive powers. Elections gave rise to parties, some of which appealed to the whole population of a colonial territory. Thus national sentiment arose some time before independence. Naturally it was not very strong, which explains some confusions resulting in disturbances, as in Cameroon, and some splitting, such as the attempted secession of Katanga and of Biafra.

Traditional African societies, with rare exceptions, cannot be transformed into modern states. Their population and their resources are insufficient to be the basis of an independent political and economic entity. If the southern Lunda wanted to unite into one state, some of those who had gone through high school would express themselves in French, others in English, and still others in Portuguese.

When they achieved political independence, the new states formed republics (except for Burundi and Lesotho). They generally adopted a parliamentary regime (in which the head of state is distinct from the head of the government) but sometimes a presidential regime (in which the head of state himself assumes the direction of the executive while parliament exercises legislative power and votes the budget). All the new states are democracies, since elections are organized, and the legitimacy of power is based on the consent of the people expressed by electoral choices.

The functioning of these regimes often tends towards strong presidential powers and a one-party system. This development has been strongly criticized by European opinion, especially in the home countries of the former colonies. It is true that such regimes do not correspond to the Western ideal of a balance of parties and respect for the right of the opposition to express itself freely. But the new governments have to face a situation in which a strong parliamentary opposition is a luxury and could be a danger.

First, feelings of national loyalty must be strongly built up so that party strife may not threaten unity. What is called "tribal particularism" is still an important force. During the colonial period it had been somewhat favored by the administration; also it was normal for Africans to remain attached to their various traditional cultures, their languages and their customs, which reminded them of a time when they had not been dominated by a foreign power. Besides these old habits, the interest of "customary authorities" required the maintenance of local particularism. These customary authorities in principle succeeded according to traditional rules of legitimacy those which controlled power in the pre-colonial societies. Actually they were often chosen by the European administrations on the basis of criteria other than those of customary succession, and they formed a lower level of colonial administration and thus enjoyed a modest but privileged position in relation to the mass of the population.

The abolition of the colonial government put this situation in danger. Naturally to protect it, the customary authorities made strong efforts to breathe new life into old loyalties, and in particular tried to find political expression for them by creating parties which identified themselves with old social and cultural entities. These regional parties threaten to disintegrate new states in which national identity is still very weak.

Secondly, a single party can fill a role in the social, political and economic education of the peasant masses, who represent a strong force of inertia. During the colonial period they were not really interested in the reason for the measures imposed upon them, some of which were directly useful to the people—for example, selective limitation of cattle herds to check the process of erosion. The governments of the new states, which demand a strong effort from all their people, must command whole-hearted even enthusiastic loyalty. They must first convince people, and to do that they must explain the process of economic life. For example, people must be made to understand that it is necessary to work harder without achieving for some considerable time a higher standard of living, because this surplus of labor is the only wealth which will make possible investment in heavy equipment which is essential for the economic growth of the nation. A political party organized in such a way that it reaches all adults divided into small groups can to some extent compensate for people's lack of education in politics and elementary economics. Unless the whole population were thus drawn into party organizations, it would be difficult to see how the inevitably conservative and suspicious masses could be mobilized and engaged in a huge collective effort.

Underdevelopment and Independence

But why is it necessary thus to mobilize energies for collective effort when political independence has been obtained? Is the battle not over?

The governments of the new states do not think that their achievement of independence, ratified by their entry into the United Nations Organization, is the end of decolonization. They still have to get out of the condition of technical and economic inferiority which is called underdevelopment. Claude Levy lists eleven criteria of underdevelopment, such as high infant mortality, lack of hygiene, illiteracy, etc. Charles Bettelheim's more synthetic idea suggests at the same time the cause and the cure. A country is underdeveloped if the majority of its population enjoys a standard of living lower than the average attained in industrialized countries, that is, countries in which less than half the population is engaged in agriculture.

And indeed industrialization seems to the African governments to be the essential means by which the standard of living of what are called the "advanced" countries may be attained. But industrial techniques, as we have shown, were introduced and made progress during the colonial period, and yet did not succeed in bringing the colonies into the category of developed countries. Therefore, it seems that industrial techniques are not sufficient in themselves but must be accompanied by a certain economic organization, different from that which prevailed in the colonial period.

That organization, as we know, implied economic dependence, different from but parallel with political dependence. The colonial enterprises were foreign in their capital, their boards of directors, their managerial personnel and their upper level technicians. They were native only in their skilled or semi-skilled workers and their raw materials. These enterprises were organized, as necessarily in a system of private capitalism, to obtain the highest possible profits. This extremely high yield, which attracted investments, was due to the low level of wages compared to that of workers in similar industries in western Europe and North America, to the richness of the mines, and to the relatively small taxes imposed by the colonial governments. The capital was foreign, the profits were taken out of the country and were only reinvested in so far as further profits, just as high, could be expected.

Another mark of economic dependence is that there is no interest in creating a varied total economy with complementary sectors. Anyway, who would care about such matters? Not the colonial authorities, who were there only to represent the government of their home countries; not the home governments, subject to pressures from powerful groups of interests and not required to consider the opinion of African "subjects," since Africans were not voters; and not even the Africans, since they did not participate in the government of their own country. Consequently only the most profitable sectors were developed, especially mining. Of course the primary processing of the minerals was more and more frequently carried out on the spot, but secondary industries, which transform one product into another, were much less widespread. This industrial anarchy makes an economy very vulnerable, for if it exports only a few products it is at the mercy of a drop in their price in the world market. The same is true of large, world-wide plantation enterprises, which often grow only one crop: coffee, cocoa, pyrethrum, etc. Thus the prosperity of a country can be destroyed by commercial fluctuations entirely outside the control of the region which suffers from them.

Despite these features, the colonial economy did have some favorable effects on the standard of living of African populations. We know that the Mining Union of Upper Katanga paid a third of the budget of the Belgian Congo. But these same features explain why colonial industrialization did not bring any colony out of the situation of underdevelopment. Thus it is not enough for the independent states to intensify industrialization in the same economic framework; they must work out a new system of economic independence and redirect the old ones, within it.

Economic Independence

The economic independence of a new state which, of course, is never complete presupposes that the country possesses its own resources of energy, industrial equipment for extracting and processing mineral wealth, manufacturing industries, a varied agriculture capable of feeding its population, and products for export; it also presupposes that the country as a whole can exercise effective control over the use of its income and especially over its reinvestment. These requirements, of which the African governments are well aware, are not easily realizable.

The first obstacle is the colonial economic structure whose orientation towards profit for foreigners has not been modified by the attainment of political independence. And the international power of European and American interest groups is used to safeguard this structure. Alvin W. Wolfe's analysis of the governing bodies of mining companies of eastern and southern Africa, and the participation of each in the capitalization of the others, shows that they form a chain which completely controls all mining industry, from Katanga to the Cape, not counting the many enterprises in transportation, electricity, chemical products and even cotton, which are affiliated with these mining companies. It is clear that these enterprises, closely interconnected on the financial level, exercise considerable power, and are ready to defend with energy the economic structures which are profitable to them and that they dispose of means of persuasion and pressure which are difficult to withstand. Another obstacle to economic independence is the new states' poverty in capital and skills. Much has been written about the emergence of a black bourgeoisie in African cities during the colonial period. If what is meant by this is a minority of Africans who enjoy an income above that of the workers and peasant villages, this is true. But most of these "bourgeois" were salaried workers (clerks, lower officials of the colonial administration, foremen, etc.) and the others were heads of very small enterprises. With a few rare exceptions, none of these had enough income to enable them to accumulate capital. Very few investments, even modest ones, few expensive buildings, little technical manpower, a very small amount of capital in the form of merchandise: such was the situation in 1950 of the "Black Brazzavilles" described by Georges Balandier. His analysis, true for the whole of central Africa, was also confirmed on a smaller scale in West Africa.

The proportion of Africans who had received complete training in technical schools or universities varied in the different colonies. Largest in French and British West Africa, small in Belgian territories, minute in Portuguese possessions, it was nowhere sufficient to fill the needs of a country in a stage of economic growth.

The new nations' main resource for building up their economy is labor. People must work harder and more efficiently and save the wealth produced by this extra work for investment, not for consumption.

With this austere outlook, we can see why we must speak of the mobilization of the energy of the whole nation, and why governments have been led to take forceful measures against the traditional chiefs, against opposition parties, against everything which could weaken the sense of national unity and the feeling of identification with the new state.

Foreign Aid and Neo-colonialism

In order to rise out of underdevelopment, this economic effort is indispensable. But it is helped by foreign aid in the form of loans or gifts of capital goods or sending out technicians and experts. The attitude of the African governments towards this aid sometimes seems very wary: acceptance with reservations, care to obtain several sources rather than only one, even refusing technicians or sending them home. This is because economic aid may tie the hands of the recipient and lead him just where he does not want to go.

There is a very strong temptation to support the investment of private foreign capital. The personal advantages to directors of enterprises are attractive. But it is doubtful whether this aid can do much to help the country towards economic development since it re-creates or perpetuates the colonial economic systems. The history of Liberia, a country which was politically independent since its foundation in 1847 and in which private American capital had been invested over a very long period, shows clearly that economic dependence has very similar effects in an independent country and in a colony. In any case, it could not be otherwise. For why should people invest in an African state, where the risks are much greater than in an old-style colony, except to receive a higher profit than could be obtained by the same investment in Western Europe or North America? And in order for profits to be higher, an economic system with colonial characteristics is necessary. This is a neo-colonialist economy, which was probably most completely realized in the secessionist "states" of Katanga and South Kasai.

The great powers which put capital goods at the disposal of the new nations do not ask a high return on their capital, but they are not indifferent to the political opinions of the African governments or their sources of supply. The competition and tensions between the Western, Soviet and Chinese blocs are at the same time an advantage and a danger to the new African states. They are an advantage because no one of these blocs wants to allow any of the others to aid exclusively; and a danger because a political alignment runs the risk of degenerating into a political neo-colonialism. Actually, the most stable of the great powers—the United States and the Soviet Union—seem to recognize that to try to tip over to their side several African states would produce an imbalance with unpredictable consequences. On the other hand, to allow the difference in prosperity between the industrialized states and those of the Third World to continue or even increase is a threat to both the United States and the Soviet Union. Under these conditions, the African statesmen can hope, through their diplomatic skill, to keep their political independence and build up an independent economic system while at the same time limiting for their peoples this austere period of intensive effort. But even with substantial economic aid, mobilization of the nation is indispensable. The common tendency of the new African states in foreign policy is, in effect, neutralism with regard to the major blocs; with regard to the system of government, one-party democracy; in economic organization, moderate socialism. This similarity of orientation, as we have seen, is not accidental, it is built into the development of the civilization of industry. This is why in order to understand its full significance, we have had to look at areas which are not usually associated with the idea of an African civilization.

Africanity and the Civilization of Industry

The civilization of industry, like the others, groups together what is common and essential to various cultures which are developing a complete pattern of adaptation to the world, starting out from an environment and a technique of production of material goods. Of course this civilization is still in the process of forming and not all the possibilities allowed by its technical basis have yet been realized, but it is already known what choices will be excluded.

Let us return to the question posed at the beginning of this chapter: what will there be specifically Africa in this modern African civilization? Will it not be identical to all the industrial societies of the world? Some people think that the introduction of industry is a phenomenon limited to the technical domain and unable to affect political or social structure or moral and judicial concepts. This is not the case. Industry cannot long accommodate the village dwelling pattern, kinship obligation, a political system based on chiefdoms, languages spoken by only a few thousand individuals. However, it can accommodate to several types of urban settlement, to several different forms of the nuclear family, to different kinds of national and local government. Within these margins of freedom, Africanity can be expressed.

For Léopold Senghor, negritude is a certain way of viewing the world and reacting to it. He sets the Black African way of thinking, "intuitive by participation" against the classic European way of thinking, "analytical by utilization," the "visual thinking" of the white European against the "involved thinking" of the Black African. He quotes with approval Jean-Paul Sartre's definition of negritude as "a certain affective attitude towards the world." Certainly, reason as such is one in the sense that its function is to apprehend the world, that is, the "objective reality" whose nature has its own laws, but its means of knowing —forms of thought—are varied and tied in with the psycho-physiology of each race. The correspondence between race and mental potentials or special features is far from being established; as we have seen in an earlier chapter, the most recent developments in physical anthropology tend to the opposite view. Thus, without casting doubt on Senghor's account of negritude, it is fitting to look at it in the light of culture and history rather than that of race. Each pre-industrial civilization of Africa has its own particular quality, but each also shows similarites to the others because all the men of Africa have faced the same reality of life on the African continent. Africanity is the special totality of values, concepts, ways of being and acting which has grown out of the long experience of many generations with this reality.

Thus communal forms of ownership and utilization of land may be selected and reinterpreted, as a function of the traditional nature of the soil, by lineage groups. The long discussions of councils of chiefs, which continued until unanimous agreement was reached, rather than division between a majority and a minority, could suggest the procedure of parliamentary meetings. The glorification of the divine power of kings certainly affects the feelings expressed for certain heads of state. But it is still too soon for these choices and reinterpretations on the basis of Africanity to be fully expressed. It is certain that the influence of the past can potentially make itself felt on the political, judicial and social levels.

The potential of Africanity is much greater in the area of philosophy, and even more in that of art. Of course a society's conception of the world and of man reflects the basic experiences of each individual, which are different in each civilization. The factory worker's contact with reality is not the same as the hunter's or the warrior's. Nature is mother and friend for the hunter; any stranger is enemy for the warrior. The natural and human environment are less important and more impersonal for the worker, but a few individuals mean more to him. So his gods are different. He will no longer fear the forces of nature; the ancestors will no longer dominate his life because the lineage has now hardly any economic or social meaning. But the gap between people's conception of the world and new experience disappears only slowly: it takes time to build a new apprehension of the world into a symbolic system.

Besides, this new conception is only partly determined by the experience of the workers' condition, which tends to become universal and to some degree uninspiring. This understanding of the world depends also on ideas which are part of the African cultural heritage. So the philosophy of the steel civilization of Africa will be marked with Africanity because it is a synthesis of a new experience—industrial life—and an ancient wisdom which has ripened slowly in contact with African realities.

In the field of artistic creation, the material used (vegetable fibers or beaten bark), the type of objects made (masks or ceremonial adzes), the subjects represented (ancestors or kings), are closely bound up with one civilization, and barely survive when the material basis of that civilization disappears. But the essential feature of an artistic tradition—its style—does not vanish. Style is the totality of forms and relations between forms which are created by a tradition, and express its special nature, and through which any man, even a stranger, may have direct, immediate, intuitive access to the special quality of a culture. Because styles are perhaps the part of culture most remote from its technico-economic basis, they tend to persist longest. That is why, through the medium of African styles—not only in the visual arts, but also in literature, music, dance, spectacle—Africanity will still express itself in complete authenticity and enrich the world with its special contribution.

In fact, the civilization of industry is no more special to Africa than are any of the other civilizations. But while the hunters of the African forests knew nothing of the hunters of the American forests, and the grain farmers knew nothing of the farmers of Asia, the men of the industrial societies know that their technology is universal, for mass communications, itself one of the aspects of the civilization of industry, make known from day to day the events that happen in all parts of the world where there are towns, aircraft and newspapers. Thus the African peoples have become aware of the world, and the world is aware of them. At last the barriers are down which have kept the greater part of Black Africa apart from the major cultural currents for centuries. Only a few peoples, privileged by their geographical position, have had access to the cultural treasure built up for many generations by a large number of societies, many of which have disappeared. The wealth of Western Europe in the eighteenth century owed much more to contributions from outside—Egypt, Greece, Rome, the Arabs, Byzantium, Persia, China, India, etc.— than to its own productiveness. Henceforth Africa too will be able to draw on the common inheritance of humanity and enrich it with new contributions, adding to its music and its visual arts, which have already become part of the heritage of all men in our time.

BIBLIOGRAPHY

GENERAL

Bascom, William R., and Herskovits, Melville J.: *Continuity and Change in African Cultures*, University of Chicago Press, Chicago, 1959.

Baumann, H., and Westermann, D.: *Les Peuples et les civilisations de l'Afrique*, Payot, Paris, 1948.

Bohannan, Paul: *Africa and Africans*, The Natural History Press, New York, 1964.

Douglas, Mary, and Kaberry, Phyllis: *Man in Africa*, Tavistock Publications, London, 1969.

Forde, Daryll: *African Worlds*, Oxford University Press, New York, 1954.

Fortes, M., and Evan-Pritchard, E. E. (eds.): *African Political Systems*, Oxford University Press, New York, 1940.

Gibbs, James L., Jr.: *Peoples of Africa*, Holt, Rinehart and Winston, New York, 1965.

Herskovits, Melville J.: *Man and His Works*, Alfred A. Knopf, New York, 1947.

Jahn, Jahnheinz: *Muntu*, Grove Press, New York, 1961.

Kimble, George H. T.: *Tropical Africa*, Doubleday, New York, 1960.

Maquet, Jacques: "Africanité traditionelle et moderne," *Présence Africaine*, Paris, 1967.

————: "African Society: Sub-Saharan Africa," *International Encyclopedia of the Social Sciences*, 1, 1968, pp. 137-55.

————: *Power and Society in Africa*, McGraw-Hill, New York, 1971.

Middleton, John (ed.): *Black Africa: Its Peoples and Their Cultures Today*, Macmillan, New York, 1970.

Murdock, George Peter: *Africa: Its Peoples and Their Culture History*, McGraw-Hill, New York, 1959.

Parrinder, Geoffrey: *African Mythology*, Paul Hamlyn, London, 1967.

Paulme, Denise: *Les civilisations africaines*, Presses Universitaires de France, Paris, 1953.

————(ed.): *Women of Tropical Africa*, University of California Press, Berkeley, 1963.

Radcliffe-Brown, A. R., and Forde, Daryll (eds.): *African Systems of Kinship and Marriage*, Oxford University Press, New York, 1950.

ART

Battis, W. W., Franz, G. H., Grossert, J. W., Junod, H. P.: *The Art of Africa*, Shuter and Shooter, Pietermaritzburg, 1958.

Beier, Ulli: *Art in Nigeria*, Cambridge University Press, London, 1960.

————: *Contemporary Art in Africa*, Pall Mall Press, London, 1968.

Breuil, H.: "Quatre cents siècles d'art pariétal," Centre d'Etudes et de Doc. préhist., Montignac, 1952.

Elisofon, Eliot: *The Sculpture of Africa*, Thames and Hudson, London, 1958.

Fagg, William, and Plass, Margaret: *African Sculpture: An Anthology*, Studio Vista Ltd., London, 1964.

Forman, W., and Dark, P.: *Benin Art*, Hamlyn-Artia, London, 1960.

Gaskin, L. J. P.: *A Bibliography of African Art*, International African Institute, London, 1965.

Herskovits, Melville J.: *The Backgrounds of African Art*, Denver Art Museum, Denver, 1945.

Himmelheber, H.: *Negerkunst und Negerkunstler*, Braunschweiger, Braunschweig, 1960.

Leiris, M., and Delange, J.: *African Art*, Thames and Hudson, London, 1968.

Olbrechts, F. M.: *Les Arts plastiques du Congo belge*, Erasme, Brussels, 1959.

Paulme, Denise: *African Sculpture*, Elek Books, London, 1962.

Présence Africaine: *L'Art nègre*, Paris, 1966.

Schmalenbach, Werner: *African Art*, Macmillan, New York, 1954.

Segy, Ladislas: *African Sculpture Speaks*, Hill and Wang, New York, 1970 (originally published 1952).

————: *African Sculpture*, Dover, New York, 1958.

Senghor, L. S.: *L'Esthétique négro-africaine*, Diogène 16, 1956, pp. 43-61.

Trowell, Margaret: *Classical African Sculpture*, Praeger, New York, 1964.

Underwood, Leon: *Bronzes of West Africa*, Tiranti, London, 1949.

————: *Figures in Wood of West Africa*, Tiranti, London, 1949.

————: *Masks of West Africa*, Tiranti, London, 1952.

Willett, F.: *Ife in the History of West African Sculpture*, Thames and Hudson, London, 1967.

EVOLUTION, PREHISTORY, LANGUAGE

Brace, C. Loring: *The Stages of Human Evolution*, Prentice-Hall, Engelwood Cliffs, 1967.

Clark, J. Desmond: *The Prehistory of Southern Africa*, Penguin Books, London, 1959.

————: *The Prehistory of Africa*, Praeger, New York, 1970.

Clarke, W. E. Le Gros: *Man-apes or Ape-men?*, Holt, Rinehart and Winston, New York, 1967.

Cole, Sonia: *The Prehistory of East Africa*, Penguin Books, London, 1954.

Coon, C. S.: *The Origin of Races*, Basic Books, New York, 1963.

Dobzhansky, Theodosius: Review of *The Origin of Races* by Carleton S. Coon, *Scientific American*, February 1963, pp. 169-72.

Fage, J. D., and Oliver, R. A.: *Papers in African Prehistory*, Cambridge University Press, Cambridge, 1970.

Greenberg, Joseph H.: *The Languages of Africa*, Indiana University Press, Bloomington, and Mouton & Co., The Hague, 1966.

Heine, Bernd: *Status and Use of African Lingua Francas*, Humanities Press, New York, 1970.

Hiernaux, J., and Maquet, E.: "Culture préhistoriques de l'âge des métaux au Ruanda-Urundi et au Kivu," Académie Royale des sciences d'Outre-mer, Brussels, 1960.

Hiernaux, Jean: *The Peoples of Africa*, Weidenfeld and Nicolson, London, 1971.

————: *La Diversité humaine en Afrique subsaharienne*, Université Libre de Bruxelles, 1968.

Leakey, R. E. F., Butzer, K. W., and Day, M. H.: "Early Homo Sapiens Remains from the Omo River Region of Southeast Ethiopia," *Nature*, 222, 1969, pp. 1132-38.

Nenquin, J.: *Excavations at Sanga*, Musée Royal d'Afrique centrale, Tervuren, 1964.

Oakley, Kenneth P.: *Man the Tool-Maker*, University of Chicago Press, Chicago, 1959.

Olderogge, Dmitri A.: "Ancient Scripts from the Heart of Africa," *The UNESCO Courier*, March 1966, pp. 25-29.

Pilbeam, David: *The Evolution of Man*, Oxford University Press, New York, 1970.

Schaller, George, B., and Lowther, Gordon R.: "The Relevance of Carnivore Behavior to the Study of Early Hominids," *Southwestern Journal of Anthropology*, Vol. 23, No. 4., Winter 1969, pp. 307-41.

Seligman, C. C.: *The Races of Africa*, Oxford University Press, London, 1966 (originally published 1930).

Vallois, Henry-V.: *Les Races humaines*, P.U.F., Paris, 1944.

Whiteley, Wilfred: *Swahili: The Rise of a National Language*, Methuen and Co., London, 1969.

HISTORY

Boxer, C. R.: "The Old Kingdom of the Congo" in R. A. Oliver (ed.): *The Dawn of African History*, Oxford University Press, London, 1968.

Caton-Thompson, G.: *Zimbabwe Culture*, Oxford University Press, London, 1931.

Collins, Robert O.: *Problems in African History*, Prentice-Hall, Engelwood Cliffs, 1968.

Curtin, Philip: *Africa Remembered*, University of Wisconsin Press, Madison, 1968.

Davidson, Basil: *A History of West Africa*, Doubleday, New York, 1966.

————: *A History of East and Central Africa*, Doubleday, New York, 1969.

————: *The Lost Cities of Africa*, Little, Brown, Boston, 1959.

————: *The African Past*, Longmans, Green, London, 1964 (Penguin Books, 1966).

Deschamps, Hubert (ed.): *Histoire générale de l'Afrique noire*, Hachette, Paris (2 vols.), 1970.

Fage, J. D.: *An Atlas of African History*, Edw. Arnold, London, 1959.

————: *An Introduction to the History of West Africa*, Cambridge University Press, Cambridge, 1969.

Hallett, Robin: *Africa to 1875*, University of Michigan Press, Ann Arbor, 1970.

Marsh, Zoe, and Kingsnorth, G. W.: *An Introduction to the History of East Africa*, Cambridge University Press, Cambridge, 1961.

Oliver, R. A.: *The Dawn of African History*, Oxford University Press, London, 1968.

———— and Atmore, A.: *Africa since 1800*, Cambridge University Press, London, 1967.

Oliver, Roland, and Fage, J. D.: *A Short History of Africa*, New York University Press, New York, 1963.

Robinson, R., and Gallagher, J.: *Africa and the Victorians*, Doubleday Anchor, New York, 1968.

Silk, Endre: *The History of Black Africa*, Akademiai Kiado, Budapest, 1966.

Vansina, J., Mauny, R., Thomas, L. V.: *The Historian in Tropical Africa*, Oxford University Press, London, 1964.

Wiedner, Donald L.: *A History of Africa South of the Sahara*, Alfred A. Knopf, New York, 1962.

CIVILIZATION OF THE BOW

Bleek, Wm. I.: *Mantis and His Friends*, Cape Town, 1923.

Ellenberger, Victor: *La Fin tragique des Bushmen*, Amiot-Dumont, Paris, 1953.

Gusinde, M.: *Die Twiden*, Vienna, 1956.

Marshall, L.: "Kung Bushmen Bands," *Africa*, 30, 1960, pp. 225-55.

Schebesta, P.: *Les Pygmées*, Gallimard, Paris, 1940.

————: *Les Pygmées du Congo belge*, Institut Royal Colonial Belge, Brussels, 1952.

Shapera, Isaac: *The Khoisan Peoples of South Africa*, Routledge, London, 1950.

Siblerhauer, G. B.: *Report to the Government of Bechuanaland on the Bushman Survey*, Gaberones, 1965.

Thomas, Elizabeth Marshall: *The Harmless People*, Alfred A. Knopf, New York, 1959.

Turnbull, Colin M.: *The Forest People*, Doubleday, New York, 1962.

————: *Wayward Servants*, Doubleday, New York, 1965.

Willcox, A. R.: *The Rock Art of South Africa*, Thomas Nelson, Johannesburg, 1963.

CIVILIZATION OF CLEARINGS

Alexandre, P., and Binet, J.: *La Groupe dit Pahouin*, Paris, 1958.

Bowen, Elenore Smith: *Return to Laughter*, Doubleday, New York, 1954.

Douglas, M.: *The Lele of the Kasai*, Oxford University Press, London, 1963.

F.A.O.: "Shifting Cultivation," *Tropical Agriculture*, 34, 1957, pp. 159-64.

Forde, D.: *Yakö Studies*, Oxford University Press, London, 1964.

Green, M. M.: *Ibo Village Affairs*, Praeger, New York, 1964.

Gourou, Pierre: *The Tropical World*, Wiley, New York, 1966.

Heusch, Luc de: *Vie quotidienne des Mongo du Kasai*, Janlet, P.: *Exploration du Monde*, Brussels, 1955.

Hulstaert, G.: *Les Mongos. Aperçu Général*, Musée Royal d'Afrique centrale, Tervuren, 1961.

Little, K. L.: *The Mende of Sierra Leone*, Routledge and Kegan Paul, London, 1951.

Paulme, Denise: *Les Gens du Riz*, Plon, Paris, 1954.

Rattray, Robert Sutherland: *Religion and Art in Ashanti*, Oxford University Press, London, 1959.

Schwab and Harley: *Tribes of the Liberian Hinterland*, University of Pennsylvania Press, Philadelphia, originally published 1947 by Peabody Museum. Papers of the Peabody Museum Vol. 31 available through Kraus Reprint Co.

Tait, D., and Middleton, J.: *Tribes without Rulers*, Routledge and Kegan Paul, 1958.

Uchendu, Victor: *The Igbo of Southeast Nigeria*, Holt, Rinehart and Winston, New York, 1965.

Van Geluwe, H.: *Les Bira et les peuplades limitrophes*, Musée Royal du Congo belge, Tervuren, 1956.

Winter, Edward H.: *Bwamba: A Structural-Functional Analysis of a Patrilineal Society*, Heffer, Cambridge, 1956.

CIVILIZATION OF GRANARIES

Balandier, Georges: *Daily Life in the Kingdom of the Kongo*, Meridian Books, New York, 1968.

Brelsford, W. V.: *The Tribes of Northern Rhodesia*, The Government Printer, Lusaka, 1956.

Cohen, Ronald: *The Kanuri of Bornu*, Holt, Rinehart and Winston, New York, 1967.

Colson, E., and Gluckman, M.: *Seven Tribes of British Central Africa*, Oxford University Press, London, 1951.

Gluckman, M.: *The Judicial Process among the Barotse of Northern Rhodesia*, The University Press, Manchester, 1955.

Hilton-Simpson, M. W.: *Land and Peoples of the Kasai*, Constable, London, 1911.

Holleman, J. F.: *Shona Customary Law*, Oxford University Press, London, 1952.

Jaspan, M. A.: *The Ila-Tonga Peoples of North-western Rhodesia*, International African Institute, London, 1953.

Lecoq, Raymond: "Les Bamiléké," *Présence Africaine*, Paris, 1953.

Mair, Lucy: *Primitive Government*, Penguin Books, London, 1962.

Mitchell, J. C.: *The Yao Village*, University Press, Manchester, 1956.

Prussin, Labelle: *Architecture in North Ghana: A Study in Forms and Functions*, University of California Press, Berkeley, 1970.

Richards, Audrey I.: *Land, Labour and Diet in Northern Rhodesia*, Oxford University Press, London, 1939.

Schlippe, P. de: *Shifting Cultivation in Africa*, Routledge and Kegan Paul, London, 1956.

Skinner, Elliot P.: *The Mossi of the Upper Volta*, Stanford University Press, Stanford, 1964.

Tempels, Placide, "Bantu Philosophy," *Présence Africaine*, Paris, 1959.

Turner, V. W.: "Lunda Rites and Ceremonies," *The Rhodes-Livingstone Papers*, University Press, London, 1939.

———: *Schism and Continuity in an African Society*, Rhodes-Livingstone Institute, Manchester University Press, Manchester, 1957.

———: *The Forest of Symbols*, Cornell University Press, Ithaca, 1967.

———: *The Drums of Affliction*, International African Institute, London, 1968.

Uchendu, Victor: *The Igbo of Southeast Nigeria*, Holt, Rinehart and Winston, 1965.

Vansina, Jan: *Kingdoms of the Savanna*, University of Wisconsin Press, Madison, 1966.

———: *Le Royaume Kuba*, Musée Royal d'Afrique centrale, Tervuren, 1964.

Verbeken, A.: *Msiri, roi du Garenganze*, Cuypers, Brussels, 1956.

Verly, R.: "Le Statuaire de pierre du Bas-Congo," *Zaire*, 9, 1955, pp. 451-528.

White, C. M. N.: *A Preliminary Survey of Luvale Rural Economy*, Rhodes-Livingstone Papers, University Press, Manchester, 1960.

———: *An Outline of Luvale Social and Political Organization*, Rhodes-Livingstone Papers, University Press, Manchester, 1960.

Whiteley, W.: *Bemba and Related Peoples of Northern Rhodesia*, International African Institute, London, 1951.

CIVILIZATION OF THE SPEAR

Beattie, John: *Bunyoro: An African Kingdom*, Holt, Rinehart and Winston, New York, 1960.

Cory, H.: *African Figurines*, Faber and Faber, London, 1956.

Crazzolara, J. P.: *The Lwoo*, 2 vol. Ed. Nigrizia, Verona, 1950.

Evans-Pritchard, E. E.: *The Nuer*, Clarendon Press, Oxford, 1940.

————: *Nuer Religion*, Clarendon Press, Oxford, 1949.

————: *The Divine Kingship of the Shilluk of the Nilotic Sudan*, Clarendon Press, Oxford, 1948.

Fallers, Lloyd: *The King's Men*, Oxford University Press, New York, 1964.

————: *Bantu Bureaucracy*, University of Chicago Press, Chicago, 1956.

Goldschmidt, Walter: *Kambuga's Cattle*, University of California Press, Berkeley, 1969.

————: *Sebei Law*, University of California Press, Berkeley, 1967.

Gulliver, P., and Gulliver P. H.: *The Central Nilo-Hamites*, International African Institute, London, 1953.

————: *The Family Herds*, Routledge and Kegan Paul, London, 1955.

Herskovits, M. J.: "The Cattle Complex in East Africa," *American Anthropologist* 28, 1926, pp. 230-380, 484-528, 633-64.

Huntingford, G. W. B.: *The Southern Nilo-Hamites*, International African Institute, London, 1953.

Irstam, T. V. H.: *The King of Ganda*, Ethnographic Museum of Sweden, Lund, 1944.

Junod, Henri A.: *The Life of a South African Tribe*, University Books, New York, 1962.

Kenyatta, Jomo: *Facing Mount Kenya*, Random House, New York, 1962.

Krige, E. J.: *The Social System of the Zulus*, Longmans, Green, London, Shuter and Shooter, Pietermaritzburg, 1957.

Kronenberg, A.: "The Longarim Favourite Beast," *Kusch* Vol. IV, Khartoum, 1961, pp. 258-77.

Kuper, Hilda: *The Swazi*, Holt, Rinehart and Winston, New York, 1963.

Lienhardt, G.: *Divinity and Experience, The Religion of the Dinka*, Clarendon Press, Oxford, 1961.

Maquet, Jacques: *The Premise of Inequality in Ruanda*, Oxford University Press, London, 1961.

Middleton, John: *The Lugbara of Uganda*, Holt, Rinehart and Winston, New York, 1965.

————: *The Study of the Lugbara: Expectations and Paradox in Anthropological Research*, Holt, Rinehart and Winston, New York, 1970.

Morris, Donald, R.: *The Washing of the Spears*, Simon and Schuster, New York, 1965.

Read, Margaret: *Children of Their Fathers: Growing Up among the Ngoni of Malawi*, Holt, Rinehart and Winston, New York, 1968.

Thomas, Elizabeth Marshall: *Warrior Herdsmen*, Alfred A. Knopf, New York, 1965.

Wilson, Monica: *Good Company*, Beacon Press, Boston, 1961.

CIVILIZATIONS OF THE CITIES

Bascom, W.: "Urbanization among the Yoruba," *The American Journal of Sociology*, 60, 1955, pp. 446-54.

————: *Ifa Divination*, Indiana University Press, Bloomington, 1969.

Beattie, John, and Middleton, John: *Spirit Mediumships and Society in Africa*, Africana Publishing Corp., New York, 1969.

Chapelle, J.: *Nomades noirs du Sahara*, Plon, Paris, 1957.

Crowder, Michael: *A Short History of Nigeria*, Praeger, New York, 1966.

Dieterlen, Germaine: *Essai sur la religion Bambara*, P.U.F., Paris, 1950.

Dike, K. O.: "Benin," *The UNESCO Courier*, October 1959.

Forde, Daryll: *The Yoruba-Speaking Peoples of Southwestern Nigeria*, International African Institute, London, 1951.

————: *Efik Traders of Old Calabar*, Oxford University Press, London, 1956.

Forde, P., Brown, P., and Armstrong, R. G.: *Peoples of the Niger-Benue Confluence*, International African Institute, London, 1955.

Forde, D., and Jones, G. I.: *The Ibo and Ibibio-Speaking Peoples of Southeastern Nigeria*, International African Institute, London, 1950.

Forde, D., and Kaberry, P.: *West African Kingdoms in the 19th Century*, International African Institute, London, 1957.

Griaule, Marcel: *Masques Dogons*, Musée de Homme, Paris, 1938.

————, and Dieterlen, Germaine: "The Dogon" in *African Worlds*, Daryll Forde, ed., Oxford University Press, New York, 1954.

Gunn, Harold D.: *Peoples of the Plateau Area of Northern Nigeria*, International African Institute, London, 1953.

Hintze, Ursula and Fritz: *Civilizations of the Old Sudan*, B. R. Gruner, Amsterdam, 1968.

Labouret, Henri: *Paysans d'Afrique occidentale*, Gallimard, Paris, 1940.

————: *Histoire des noirs d'Afrique*, P.U.F., Paris, 1950.

Lebeuf, Annie Masson-Detourbet: *Les Populations de Tchad*, International African Institute, London, P.U.F., Paris, 1950.

————: *Les Principautés Kotoko*, Paris, Editions du centre national de la recherche scientifique, 1969.

Lebeuf, Jean-Paul: *L'Habitation des Fali*, Hachette, Paris, 1961.

————: *Art ancien du Tchad*, Catalogue de l'Exposition, Grand Palais, Paris, 1962.

Lebeuf, J. P., and Masson-Detourbet, A.: *La Civilisation du Tchad*, Payot, Paris, 1950.

Lewis, I. M.: *Islam in Tropical Africa*, Oxford University Press, London, 1966.

Mauny, R.: *Tableau géographique de l'Ouest africain au moyen âge*, IFAN, Dakar, 1961.

Miner, Horace: *The Primitive City of Timbuctoo*, Doubleday, New York, 1965.

Nadel, S. F.: *A Black Byzantium*, Oxford University Press, London, 1941.

Paques, Viviana: *Les Bambara*, International African Institute, London, P.U.F. Paris, 1954.

Paulme, Denise: *Organisation sociale des Dogon*, Domat-Mont-Chrestien, Paris, 1940.

Rattray, R. S.: *Ashanti*, Oxford University Press, London, 1923.

————: *Religion and Art in Ashanti*, Oxford University Press, London, 1927, 1959.

Rouch, Jean: *Les Songhay*, International African Institute, London, P.U.F., Paris, 1954.

Ryder, A. F. C.: *Benin and the Europeans, 1485-1897*, Oxford University Press, London, 1969.

Smith, Michael G.: *Government in Zazzau*, Oxford University Press, London, 1962.

Zahan, Dominique: *Sociétés d'initiation Bambara*, Mouton, Paris, 1960.

CIVILIZATION OF INDUSTRY

Apter, David: *The Gold Coast in Transition*, Princeton University Press, Princeton, 1955.

————: *The Political Kingdom in Uganda*, Princeton University Press, Princeton, 1961.

Arikpo, Okoi: *The Development of Modern Nigeria*, Penguin Books, London, 1967.

Balandier, Georges: *Ambiguous Africa*, Meridian Books, New York, 1969.

————: *Sociology of Black Africa*, Praeger, New York, 1970.

Brausch, Georges: *Belgian Administration in the Congo*, Oxford University Press, Oxford, 1961.

Carter, Gwendolen M., (ed.): *African One-Party States*, Cornell University Press, Ithaca, 1962.

Cohen, Ronald, and Middleton, John, eds.: *From Tribe to Nation in Africa: Studies in Incorporation Processes*, Chandler, Scranton, 1970.

Coleman, James: *Nigeria: Background to Nationalism*, University of California Press, Berkeley, 1960.

Daggs, Elise: *All Africa*, Hastings House, New York, 1970.

Davidson, Basil: *The Liberation of Guiné*, Penguin Books, London, 1969.

Deschamps, H.: *Les Institutions politiques de l'Afrique noire*, P.U.F. Paris, 1962.

Fraenkel, M.: *Tribe and Class in Monrovia*, Oxford University Press, London, 1964.

Gann, L. H., and Duigan, F.: *White Settlers in Tropical Africa*, Oxford University Press, London, 1962.

Hailey, Lord: *An African Survey Revised*, Oxford University Press, New York, 1957.

Heinz, G.: *Lumumba: The Last Fifty Days*, Grove Press, New York, 1970.

Hunter, Guy: *The New Societies of Tropical Africa*, Praeger, New York, 1964.

Jaspan, M. A.: *The Ila-Tonga People of Northwestern Rhodesia*, International African Institute, London, 1952.

Kaunda, Kenneth: *Zambia: Independence and Beyond*, Nelson, London, 1966.

Kidd, Dudley: *Kafir Socialism*, Negro Universities Press, New York, 1969.

Kraph-Askari, E.: *Yoruba Towns and Cities*, Clarendon Press, Oxford, 1969.

Kuper, Leo: *An African Bourgeoisie*, Yale University Press, New Haven, 1965.

Lefever, Ernest W.: *Spear and Scepter,* The Brookings Institution, Washington, D.C., 1970.

————: *Crisis in the Congo,* The Brookings Institution, Washington, D.C., 1965.

Legum, Colin, and Drysdale, John: *Africa: Contemporary Record,* Africa Research Ltd., Exeter, 1970.

Levy, Claude: Les critères du sous-developpement. *Le "Tiers-monde,"* Balandier, G., and Sauvy, A., 1961, pp. 137-48.

Little, Kenneth L.: *West African Urbanization,* Cambridge University Press, Cambridge, 1966.

Markovitz, Irving Leonard: *Leopold Sedar Senghor and the Politics of Negritude,* Atheneum, New York, 1969.

Mitchell, J.: *Kalela Dance,* University Press, Manchester, 1956.

Nkrumah, Kwame: *I Speak of Freedom,* Praeger, New York, 1961.

————: *Consciencism,* Heinemann, London, 1964, Monthly Review Press, New York, 1970.

O'Brien, Conor Cruise: *To Katanga and Back,* Grosset & Dunlap, New York, 1962.

Ojukwu, C. Idimegwa: *Biafra,* Harper and Row, New York, 1969.

Pieterse, Cosmo, and Munro, Donald, (eds.): *Protest and Power in Black Africa,* Heinemann, London, 1969.

Post, Ken: *The New States of West Africa,* Penguin Books, London, 1964.

Powdermaker, Hortense: *Coppertown: Changing Africa,* Harper and Row, New York, 1962.

Reining, Conrad C.: *The Zande Scheme. An Anthropological Case Study of Economic Development in Africa,* Northwestern University Press, Evanston, 1966.

Rotberg, Robert I., and Mazrui, Ali A., (eds.): *Protest and Power in Black Africa,* Oxford University Press, New York, 1970.

Senghor, Léopold Sédar: *On African Socialism,* trans. and with an Introduction by Mercer Cook, Praeger, New York (1961) 1964.

Singleton, F. Seth, and Shingler, John: *Africa in Perspective,* Hayden Book Company, New York, 1967.

Southall, A. W.: *Social Change in Modern Africa,* Oxford University Press, London, 1963.

Touré, S.: *L'Expérience guinéenne et l'unité africaine,* Paris, 1961.

Tuden, Arthur, and Plotnicov, Leonard, eds.: *Social Stratification in Africa,* Free Press (Macmillan), New York, 1970.

Van den Berghe, Pierre: *Africa: Social Problems of Change and Conflict,* Chandler Publishing Co., San Francisco, 1965.

Wallerstein, Immanuel: *Africa: The Politics of Independence*, Alfred
      A. Knopf, New York, 1961.
————: *Africa: The Politics of Unity*, Random House, New York,
      1967.
————: *Social Change*, Wiley, New York, 1966.
Wolfe, A. W.: "The Team Rules Mining in South Africa," *Toward
      Freedom*, Vol. 11, no. 1, 1962.
Young: Crawford: *Politics in the Congo*, Princeton University Press,
      Princeton, 1965.

INDEX